T0221199

PyTorch Pocket Reference
*Building and Deploying
Deep Learning Models*

Joe Papa

Beijing · Boston · Farnham · Sebastopol · Tokyo

PyTorch Pocket Reference

by Joe Papa

Published by O'Reilly Media, Inc., 1005 Gravenstein Highway North, Sebastopol, CA 95472.

O'Reilly books may be purchased for educational, business, or sales promotional use. Online editions are also available for most titles (*http://oreilly.com*). For more information, contact our corporate/institutional sales department: 800-998-9938 or *corporate@oreilly.com*.

Acquisitions Editor: Rebecca Novack
Development Editor: Jeff Bleiel
Production Editor: Beth Kelly
Copyeditor: Piper Editorial Consulting, LLC
Proofreader: Rachel Head
Indexer: Potomac Indexing, LLC
Interior Designer: David Futato
Cover Designer: Karen Montgomery
Illustrator: Kate Dullea

May 2021:   First Edition

Revision History for the First Edition

    2021-05-11:   First Release

See *https://oreil.ly/9781492090007* for release details.

978-1-492-09000-7

[LSI]

Table of Contents

Preface

We are living in exciting times! Some of us have been fortunate to have lived through huge advances in technology—the invention of the personal computer, the dawn of the internet, the proliferation of cell phones, and the advent of social media. And now, major breakthroughs are happening in AI!

It's exciting to watch and be a part of this change. I think we're just getting started, and it's amazing to think of how the world might change over the next decade. How great it is that we're living during these times and can participate in the expansion of AI?

PyTorch has, no doubt, enabled some of the finest advances in deep learning and AI. It's free to download and use, and with it anyone with a computer or internet connection can run AI experiments. In addition to more comprehensive references like this one, there are many free and inexpensive training courses, blog articles, and tutorials that can help you. Anyone can get started using PyTorch for machine learning and AI.

Who Should Read This Book

This book is written for both beginners and advanced users interested in machine learning and AI. It will help to have some experience writing Python code and a basic understanding of data science and machine learning.

If you're just getting started in machine learning, this book will help you learn the basics of PyTorch and provide some simple examples. If you've been using another framework, such as TensorFlow, Caffe2, or MXNet, the book with help you become familiar with the PyTorch API and its programming mindset so you can expand your skillset.

If you've been using PyTorch for a while, this book will help you expand your knowledge on advanced topics like acceleration and optimization and provide a quick-reference resource while you use PyTorch for your day-to-day development.

Why I Wrote This Book

Learning and mastering PyTorch can be very exciting. There's so much to explore! When I first started learning PyTorch, I wished I had a single resource that would teach me everything. I wanted something that would give me a good high-level look at what PyTorch had to offer, but also would provide examples and enough details when I needed to dig deeper.

There are some really good books and courses on PyTorch, but they often focus on tensors and training for deep learning models. The PyTorch online documentation is really good, too, and provides a lot of details and examples; however, I found using it was often cumbersome. I kept having to click around to learn or Google what I needed to know. I needed a book on my desk that I could earmark and reference as I was coding.

My goal is that this will be the ultimate PyTorch reference for you. In addition to reading through it to get a high-level understanding of the PyTorch resources available to you, I hope that you earmark the key sections for your development work and keep it on your desk. That way if you forget something, you can get the answer right away. If you prefer ebooks or online books, You can bookmark this book online. However you may use it, I hope the book helps you create some amazing new technology with PyTorch!

Navigating This Book

If you're just beginning to learn PyTorch, you should start at Chapter 1 and read each chapter in sequence. The chapters move from beginner to advanced topics. If you already have some experience with PyTorch, you might want to jump around to the topics that interest you the most. Don't forget to check out Chapter 8 on the PyTorch Ecosystem. You're bound to discover something new!

This book is roughly organized as follows:

- Chapter 1 gives a brief introduction to PyTorch, helps you set up your development environment, and provides a fun example for you to try yourself.

- Chapter 2 covers the tensor, PyTorch's fundamental building block. It's the foundation for everything in PyTorch.

- Chapter 3 gives you a comprehensive look at how you can use PyTorch for deep learning, and Chapter 4 provides example reference designs so you can see PyTorch in action.

- Chapters 5 and 6 cover more advanced topics. Chapter 5 shows you how you can customize PyTorch components for your own work, while Chapter 6 shows you how to accelerate training and optimize your models.

- Chapter 7 shows you how you can deploy PyTorch to production via local machines, cloud servers, and mobile or edge devices.

- Chapter 8 guides you in where to go next by introducing the PyTorch Ecosystem, describing popular packages, and listing additional training resources.

Conventions Used in This Book

The following typographical conventions are used in this book:

Italic

> Indicates new terms, URLs, email addresses, filenames, and file extensions.

`Constant width`

> Used for program listings, as well as within paragraphs to refer to program elements such as variable or function names, databases, data types, environment variables, statements, and keywords.

`Constant width bold`

> Shows commands or other text that should be typed literally by the user. Additionally, bold is used for emphasis in functions in tables.

`Constant width italic`

> Shows text that should be replaced with user-supplied values or by values determined by context. Additionally, italic transforms listed in tables are currently not supported by TorchScript.

Using Code Examples

Supplemental material (code examples, exercises, etc.) is available for download at *https://github.com/joe-papa/pytorch-book*.

If you have a technical question or a problem using the code examples, please email *bookquestions@oreilly.com*.

This book is here to help you get your job done. In general, if example code is offered with this book, you may use it in your programs and documentation. You do not need to contact us for permission unless you're reproducing a significant portion of the code. For example, writing a program that uses several chunks of code from this book does not require permission. Selling or distributing examples from O'Reilly books does require permission. Answering a question by citing this book and quoting example code does not require permission. Incorporating a significant amount of example code from this book into your product's documentation does require permission.

We appreciate, but generally do not require, attribution. An attribution usually includes the title, author, publisher, and ISBN. For example: "*PyTorch Pocket Reference* by Joe Papa (O'Reilly). Copyright 2021 Mobile Insights Technology Group, LLC, 978-1-492-09000-7."

If you feel your use of code examples falls outside fair use or the permission given above, feel free to contact us at *permissions@oreilly.com*.

O'Reilly Online Learning

For more than 40 years, *O'Reilly Media* has provided technology and business training, knowledge, and insight to help companies succeed.

Our unique network of experts and innovators share their knowledge and expertise through books, articles, and our online learning platform. O'Reilly's online learning platform gives you on-demand access to live training courses, in-depth learning paths, interactive coding environments, and a vast collection of text and video from O'Reilly and 200+ other publishers. For more information, visit *http://oreilly.com*.

How to Contact Us

Please address comments and questions concerning this book to the publisher:

O'Reilly Media, Inc.
1005 Gravenstein Highway North
Sebastopol, CA 95472
800-998-9938 (in the United States or Canada)
707-829-0515 (international or local)

707-829-0104 (fax)

We have a web page for this book, where we list errata, examples, and any additional information. You can access this page at *https://oreil.ly/PyTorch-pocket*.

Email *bookquestions@oreilly.com* to comment or ask technical questions about this book.

For news and information about our books and courses, visit *http://oreilly.com*.

Find us on Facebook: *http://facebook.com/oreilly*

Follow us on Twitter: *http://twitter.com/oreillymedia*

Watch us on YouTube: *http://youtube.com/oreillymedia*

Acknowledgments

As a reader, I'm often amazed when reading the acknowledgments from other authors. Writing a book is no small task, and writing a good book requires the support of many people. Reading the acknowledgments is a constant reminder that we cannot do it alone.

I am thankful for the support and encouragement of my friend, Matt Kirk, whom I met at an O'Reilly conference years ago. His shared passion for personal development is an inspiration to create books and courses and help others reach their full potential, both personally and professionally. Our weekly Zoom chats and self-help projects during the pandemic definitely helped me keep my sanity. Without Matt, this book would not have been possible.

I'd like to thank Rebecca Novack for suggesting the project and taking a chance on me, as well as the staff at O'Reilly for making this project happen.

Writing a book requires effort, but writing a good book requires dedicated reviewers who care about the readers. I'd like to thank Mike Drob, Axel Sirota, and Jeff Bleiel for taking the time to review the book and provide countless suggestions. Mike's suggestions added many practical resources that I would have otherwise overlooked. He made sure that we were using state-of-the-art tools and best practices you won't find in online documentation.

Axel's attention to detail is incredible. I'm grateful for his encouragement and efforts to review the code and technical details in this book. Jeff is an amazing editor. I'm grateful for his suggestions on the sequencing and flow of the book. He's significantly helped me become a better author.

PyTorch is truly a community project. I am grateful for those at Facebook and the over 1,700 contributors that have developed this machine learning framework. I'd especially like to thank those who have created documentation and tutorials that help others like myself learn PyTorch quickly.

Some individuals whose work has helped me the most include Suraj Subramanian, Seth Juarez, Cassie Breviu, Dmitry Soshnikov, Ari Bornstein, Soumith Chintala, Justin Johnson, Jeremy Howard, Rachel Thomas, Francisco Ingham, Sasank Chilamkurthy, Nathan Inkawhich, Sean Robertson, Ben Trevett, Avinash Sajjanshetty, James Reed, Michael Suo, Michela Paganini, Shen Li, Séb Arnold, Rohan Varma, Pritam Damania, Jeff Tang, and the countless bloggers and YouTubers on the subject of PyTorch.

I'm grateful to Manbir Gulati for introducing me to PyTorch and to Rob Miller for giving me the opportunity to lead AI projects with PyTorch. I also appreciated sharing deep learning ideas for this book with my friend Isaac Privitera.

Of course, I couldn't have accomplished anything in life without the hard work and dedication of my mom, Grace, who brought us from humble beginnings to give me and my brother a chance at life. I miss her every day.

Special thanks to my brother, Vinnie, who was a big help in completing my home projects, giving me more time to write. I appreciate my stepfather, Lou, for his encouragement while I was writing the book. I'd also like to thank my kids, Savannah, Caroline, and George, for being patient and understanding when daddy had to work.

Lastly, I'd like to thank my wife, Emily. She has always endlessly supported my ideas and dreams throughout my life. As I tackled the task of writing this book, of course, I relied on her once again. Caring for our three children and taking on new responsibilities during the pandemic has been a tall order.

Still, she has been the support I needed to complete my writing. In fact, while writing this book, we found out that we're expecting, and our fourth child is on his way! My wife does it all with a smile and a joke (which are often at my expense), and I love her for it.

## CHAPTER 1

An Introduction to PyTorch

PyTorch is one of the most popular deep learning Python libraries, and it is widely used by the AI research community. Many developers and researchers use PyTorch to accelerate deep learning research experimentation and prototyping.

In this chapter, I will give you a brief introduction to what PyTorch is and some of the features that make it popular. I'll also show you how to install and set up your PyTorch development environment on your local machine and in the cloud. By the end of this chapter, you will be able to verify that PyTorch is properly installed and run a simple PyTorch program.

What Is PyTorch?

The PyTorch library is primarily developed by Facebook's AI Research Lab (FAIR) and is free and open source software with over 1,700 contributors. It allows you to easily run array-based calculations, build dynamic neural networks, and perform autodifferentiation in Python with strong graphics processing unit (GPU) acceleration—all important features required for deep learning research. Although some use it for accelerated tensor computing, most use it for deep learning development.

PyTorch's simple and flexible interface enables fast experimentation. You can load data, apply transforms, and build models with a few lines of code. Then, you have the flexibility to write customized training, validation, and test loops and deploy trained models with ease.

It has a strong ecosystem and a large user community, including universities like Stanford and companies such as Uber, NVIDIA, and Salesforce. In 2019, PyTorch dominated machine learning and deep learning conference proceedings: 69% of the Conference on Computer Vision and Pattern Recognition (CVPR) proceedings used PyTorch, over 75% of both the Association for Computational Linguistics (ACL) and the North American Chapter of the ACL (NAACL) used it, and over 50% of the International Conference on Learning Representations (ICLR) and the International Conference on Machine Learning (ICML) used it as well. There are also over 60,000 repositories on GitHub related to PyTorch.

Many developers and researchers use PyTorch to accelerate deep learning research experimentation and prototyping. Its simple Python API, GPU support, and flexibility make it a popular choice among academic and commercial research organizations. Since being open sourced in 2018, PyTorch has reached a stable release and can be easily installed on Windows, Mac, and Linux operating systems. The framework continues to expand rapidly and now facilitates deployment to production environments in the cloud and mobile platforms.

Why Use PyTorch?

If you're studying machine learning, conducting deep learning research, or building AI systems, you'll probably need to use a deep learning framework. A deep learning framework makes it easy to perform common tasks such data loading, preprocessing, model design, training, and deployment. PyTorch has become very popular with the academic and research communities due to its simplicity, flexibility, and Python interface. Here are some reasons to learn and use PyTorch:

PyTorch is popular
> Many companies and research organizations use PyTorch as their main deep learning framework. In fact, some companies have built their custom machine learning tools on top of PyTorch. As a result, PyTorch skills are in demand.

PyTorch is supported by all major cloud platforms, such as Amazon Web Services (AWS), Google Cloud Platform (GCP), Microsoft Azure, and Alibaba Cloud
> You can spin up a virtual machine with PyTorch preloaded for frictionless development. You can use prebuilt Docker images, perform large-scale training on cloud GPU platforms, and run models at production scale.

PyTorch is supported by Google Colaboratory and Kaggle Kernels
> You can run PyTorch code in a browser with no installation or configuration needed. You can compete in Kaggle competitions by running PyTorch directly in your kernel.

PyTorch is mature and stable
> PyTorch is regularly maintained and is now beyond release 1.8.

PyTorch supports CPU, GPU, TPU, and parallel processing
> You can accelerate your training and inference using GPUs and TPUs. Tensor processing units (TPUs) are AI-accelerated application-specific integrated circuits (ASIC) chips that were developed by Google to provide an alternative to GPUs for NN hardware acceleration. With parallel processing, you can apply preprocessing on your CPU while training a model on the GPU or TPU.

PyTorch supports distributed training
> You can train neural networks over multiple GPUs on multiple machines.

PyTorch supports deployment to production
> With the newer TorchScript and TorchServe features, you can easily deploy models to production environments including cloud servers.

PyTorch is beginning to support mobile deployment
> Although it's currently experimental, you can now deploy models to iOS and Android devices.

PyTorch has a vast ecosystem and set of open source libraries
> Libraries such as Torchvision, fastai, and PyTorch Lightning extend capabilities and support specific fields like natural olanguage processing (NLP) and computer vision.

PyTorch also has a C++ frontend
> Although I will focus on the Python interface in this book, PyTorch also supports a frontend C++ interface. If you need to build high-performance, low-latency, or bare-metal applications, you can write them in C++ using the same design and architecture as the Python API.

PyTorch supports the Open Neural Network Exchange (ONNX) format natively
> You can easily export your models to ONNX format and use them with ONNX-compatible platforms, runtimes, or visualizers.

PyTorch has a large community of developers and user forums
> There are more than 38,000 users on the PyTorch forum, and it's easy to get support or post questions to the community by visiting the PyTorch Discussion Forum (*https://pytorch.tips/discuss*).

Getting Started

If you are familiar with PyTorch, you may already have installed it and set up your development environment. If not, I will show you some options to do so in this section. The fastest way to get started is to use Google Colaboratory (or *Colab*). Google Colab is a free cloud-based development environment similar to Jupyter Notebook and comes with PyTorch already installed. Colab comes with free limited GPU support and interfaces nicely with Google Drive for saving and sharing notebooks.

If you don't have internet access, or you want to run the PyTorch code on your own hardware, then I will show you how to install PyTorch on a local machine. You can install PyTorch on Windows, Linux, and macOS operating systems. I recommend that you have an NVIDIA GPU for acceleration, but it is not required.

Lastly, you may want to develop PyTorch code using a cloud platform like AWS, Azure, or GCP. If you would like to use a cloud platform, I will show you the options to quickly get started on each platform.

Running in Google Colaboratory

With Google Colab, you can write and execute Python and PyTorch code in your browser. You can save files directly to your Google Drive account and easily share your work with others. To get started, visit the Google Colab website (*https://pytorch.tips/colab*), as shown in Figure 1-1.

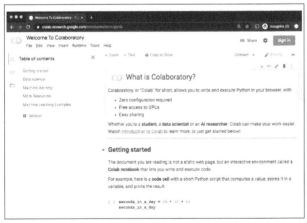

Figure 1-1. Google Colaboratory welcome page

If you are already signed into your Google account, you will get a pop-up window. Click New Notebook in the bottom-right corner. If the pop-up window does not appear, click File and select New Notebook from the menu. You will be prompted to sign in or create a Google account, as shown in Figure 1-2.

Figure 1-2. Google sign in

To verify your configuration, import the PyTorch library, print the installed version, and check if you are using a GPU, as shown in Figure 1-3.

Figure 1-3. Verify PyTorch installation in Google Colaboratory

By default, our Colab notebook does not use a GPU. You will need to select Change Runtime Type from the Runtime menu, then select GPU from the "Hardware accelerator" drop-down menu and click Save, as shown in Figure 1-4.

Figure 1-4. Use a GPU in Google Colaboratory

Now run the cell again by selecting the cell and pressing Shift-Enter. You should see `True` as the output of `is_available()`, as shown in Figure 1-5.

Figure 1-5. Verify GPU is active in Google Colaboratory

NOTE

Google offers a paid version called Colab Pro that provides faster GPUs, longer runtimes, and more memory. For the examples in this book, the free version of Colab should be sufficient.

Now you have verified that PyTorch is installed, and you also know the version. You have also verified that you have a GPU available and that the proper drivers are installed and operating correctly. Next, I will show you how to verify your PyTorch on a local machine.

Running on a Local Computer

You may want to install PyTorch on a local machine or your own server under certain conditions. For example, you may want to work with local storage, or use your own GPU or faster GPU hardware, or you may not have internet access. Running PyTorch does not require a GPU, but one would be needed to run GPU acceleration. I recommend using an NVIDIA GPU as PyTorch is closely tied to the Compute Unified Device Architecture (CUDA) drivers for GPU support.

WARNING

Check your GPU and CUDA version first! PyTorch only supports specific GPU and CUDA versions, and many Mac computers use non-NVIDIA GPUs. If you are using a Mac, verify that you have an NVIDIA GPU by clicking the Apple icon on the menu bar, selecting "About This Mac," and clicking the Displays tab. If you see an NVIDIA GPU on your Mac and want to use it, you'll have to build PyTorch from scratch. If you do not see an NVIDIA GPU, you should use the CPU-only version of PyTorch or choose another computer with a different OS.

The PyTorch website offers a convenient browser tool for installation (*https://pytorch.tips/install-local*), as shown in Figure 1-6. Select the latest stable build, your OS, your preferred Python package manager (Conda is recommended), the Python language, and your CUDA version. Execute the command line and follow the instructions for your configuration.

Note the prerequisites, installation instructions, and verification methods.

Figure 1-6. PyTorch online installation configuration tool

You should be able to run the verification code snippet in your favorite IDE (Jupyter Notebook, Microsoft Visual Studio Code, PyCharm, Spyder, etc.) or from the terminal. Figure 1-7 shows how to verify that the correct version of PyTorch is installed from a terminal on a Mac. The same commands can be used to verify this in a Windows or Linux terminal as well.

Figure 1-7. PyTorch verification using a Mac terminal

Running on Cloud Platforms

If you're familiar with cloud platforms like AWS, GCP, or Azure, you can run PyTorch in the cloud. Cloud platforms provide powerful hardware and infrastructure for training and deploying deep learning models. Remember that using cloud services, especially GPU instances, incurs additional costs. To get started, follow the instructions in the online PyTorch cloud setup guide (*https://pytorch.tips/start-cloud*) for your platform of interest.

Setting up your cloud environment is beyond the scope of this book, but I'll summarize the available options. Each platform offers a virtual machine instance as well as managed services to support PyTorch development.

Running on AWS

AWS offers multiple options to run PyTorch in the cloud. If you prefer a fully managed service, you can use AWS Sage-Maker, or if you'd rather manage your own infrastructure, you can use AWS Deep Learning Amazon Machine Images (AMIs) or Containers:

Amazon SageMaker
> This is a fully managed service to train and deploy models. You can run Jupyter Notebooks from the dashboard and use the SageMaker Python SDK to train and deploy models in the cloud. You can run your notebooks on a dedicated GPU instance.

AWS Deep Learning AMIs
> These are preconfigured virtual machine environments. You can choose the Conda AMI, which has many libraries (including PyTorch) preinstalled, or you can use the base AMI if you'd prefer a clean environment to set up private repositories or custom builds.

AWS Deep Learning Containers
> These are Docker images that come preinstalled with PyTorch. They enable you to skip the process of building

and optimizing your environment from scratch and are mainly used for deployment.

For more detailed information on how to get started, review the "Getting Started with PyTorch on AWS" instructions (*https://pytorch.tips/start-aws*).

Running on Microsoft Azure

Azure also offers multiple options to run PyTorch in the cloud. You can develop PyTorch models using a fully managed service called Azure Machine Learning, or you can run Data Science Virtual Machines (DSVMs) if you prefer to manage your own infrastructure:

Azure Machine Learning
This is an enterprise-grade machine learning service for building and deploying models. It includes a drag-and-drop designer and MLOps capabilities to integrate with existing DevOps processes.

DSVMs
These are preconfigured virtual machine environments. They come preinstalled with PyTorch and other deep learning frameworks as well as development tools like Jupyter Notebook and VS Code.

For more detailed information on how to get started, review the Azure Machine Learning documentation (*https://pytorch.tips/azure*).

Running on Google Cloud Platform

GCP also offers multiple options to run PyTorch in the cloud. You can develop PyTorch models using the managed service, called AI Platform Notebooks, or run Deep Learning VM images if you prefer to manage your own infrastructure:

AI Platform Notebooks

This is a managed service whose integrated JupyterLab environment allows you to create preconfigured GPU instances.

Deep Learning VM images

These are preconfigured virtual machine environments. They come preinstalled with PyTorch and other deep learning frameworks as well as development tools.

For more detailed information on how to get started, review the instructions at Google Cloud "AI and Machine Learning Products" (*https://pytorch.tips/google-cloud*).

Verifying Your PyTorch Environment

Whether you use Colab, your local machine, or your favorite cloud platform, you should verify that PyTorch is properly installed and check to see if you have a GPU available. You've already seen how to do this in Colab. To verify that PyTorch is properly installed, use the following code snippet. The code imports the PyTorch library, prints the version, and checks to see if a GPU is available:

```
import torch
print(torch.__version__)
print(torch.cuda.is_available())
```

WARNING

You import the library using `import torch`, not `import pytorch`. PyTorch is originally based on the `torch` library, an open source machine learning framework based on the C and Lua programming languages. Keeping the library named `torch` allows Torch code to be reused with a more efficient PyTorch implementation.

A Fun Example

Now that you have verified that your environment is configured properly, let's code up a fun example to show some of the features of PyTorch and demonstrate best practices in machine learning. In this example, we'll build a classic image classifier that will attempt to identify an image's content based on 1,000 possible classes or choices.

You can access this example from the book's GitHub repository (*https://github.com/joe-papa/pytorch-book*) and follow along. Try running the code in Google Colab, on your local machine, or on a cloud platform like AWS, Azure, or GCP. Don't worry about understanding all of the concepts of machine learning. We'll cover them in more detail throughout the book.

NOTE

In practice, you will import all the necessary libraries at the beginning of your code. However, in this example, we will import the libraries as they are used so you can see which libraries are needed for each task.

First, let's select an image we'd like to classify. In this example, we'll choose a nice fresh, hot cup of coffee. Use the following code to download the coffee image to your local environment:

```
import urllib.request

url = url = 'https://pytorch.tips/coffee'
fpath = 'coffee.jpg'
urllib.request.urlretrieve(url, fpath)
```

Notice that the code uses the `urllib` library's `urlretrieve()` function to get an image from the web. We rename the file to *coffee.jpg* by specifying `fpath`.

Next, we read our local image using the Pillow library (PIL):

```
import matplotlib.pyplot as plt
from PIL import Image

img = Image.open('coffee.jpg')
plt.imshow(img)
```

Figure 1-8 shows what our image looks like. We can use mat plotlib's imshow() function to display the image on our system, as shown in the preceding code.

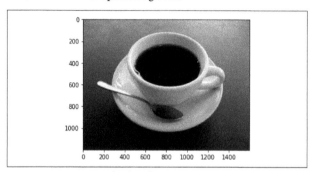

Figure 1-8. Input image for classifier

Notice we haven't used PyTorch yet. Here's where things get exciting. Next, we are going to pass our image into a pretrained image classification neural network (NN)—but before we do so, we'll need to *preprocess* our image. Preprocessing data is very common in machine learning since the NN expects the input to meet certain requirements.

In our example, the image data is an RGB 1600 × 1200-pixel JPEG-formatted image. We need to apply a series of preprocessing steps, called *transforms*, to convert the image into the proper format for the NN. We do this using Torchvision in the following code:

```
import torch
from torchvision import transforms

transform = transforms.Compose([
  transforms.Resize(256),
  transforms.CenterCrop(224),
  transforms.ToTensor(),
```

```
transforms.Normalize(
    mean=[0.485, 0.456, 0.406],
    std=[0.229, 0.224, 0.225])])

img_tensor = transform(img)
print(type(img_tensor), img_tensor.shape)
# out:
# <class 'torch.tensor'> torch.Size([3, 224, 224])
```

We use the Compose() transform to define a series of transforms
used to preprocess our image. First, we need to resize and crop
the image to fit within the NN. The image is currently in PIL
format, since that's how we read it earlier. But our NN requires
a tensor input, so we convert the PIL image to a tensor.

Tensors are the fundamental data objects in PyTorch, and we'll
spend the entire next chapter exploring them. You can think of
tensors like NumPy arrays or numerical arrays with a bunch of
extra features. For now, we'll just convert our image to a tensor
array of numbers to get it ready.

We apply one more transform, called Normalize(), to rescale
the range of pixel values between 0 and 1. The values for the
mean and standard deviation (std) were precomputed based on
the data used to train the model. Normalizing the image
improves the accuracy of the classifier.

Finally, we call transform(img) to apply all the transforms to
the image. As you can see, img_tensor is a 3 × 224 × 224
torch.Tensor representing a 3-channel image of 224 × 224
pixels.

Efficient machine learning processes data in batches, and our
model will expect a batch of data. However, we only have one
image, so we'll need to create a batch of size 1, as shown in the
following code:

```
batch = img_tensor.unsqueeze(0)
print(batch.shape)
# out: torch.Size([1, 3, 224, 224])
```

We use PyTorch's unsqueeze() function to add a dimension to
our tensor and create a batch of size 1. Now we have a tensor of
size 1 × 3 × 224 × 224, which represents a batch size of 1 and 3

channels (RGB) of 224 × 224 pixels. PyTorch provides a lot of useful functions like unsqueeze() to manipulate tensors, and we'll explore many of them in the next chapter.

Now our image is ready for our classifier NN! We'll use a famous image classifier called AlexNet. AlexNet won the ImageNet Large Scale Visual Recognition Challenge in 2012. It's easy to load this model using Torchvision, as shown in the following code:

```
from torchvision import models

model = models.alexnet(pretrained=True)
```

We're going to use a pretrained model here, so we don't need to train it. The AlexNet model has been pretrained with millions of images and does a pretty good job at classifying images. Let's pass in our image and see how it does:

```
device = "cuda" if torch.cuda.is_available() else "cpu"
print(device)
# out(results will vary): cpu

model.eval()
model.to(device)
y = model(batch.to(device))
print(y.shape)
# out: torch.Size([1, 1000])
```

GPU acceleration is a key benefit of PyTorch. In the first line, we use PyTorch's cuda.is_available() function to see if our machine has a GPU. This is a very common line of PyTorch code, and we'll explore GPUs further in Chapters 2 and 6. We're only classifying one image, so we don't need a GPU here, but if we had a huge batch having a GPU might help speed things up.

The model.eval() function configures our AlexNet model for inference or prediction (as opposed to training). Certain components of the model are only used during training, and we don't want to use them here. The use of model.to(device) and batch.to(device) sends our model and input data to the GPU if available, and executing model(batch.to(device)) runs our classifier.

The output, y, consists of a batch of 1,000 outputs. Since our batch contains only one image, the first dimension is 1 while the number of classes is 1000, one value for each class. The higher the value, the more likely it is that the image contains that class. The following code finds the winning class:

```
y_max, index = torch.max(y,1)
print(index, y_max)
# out: tensor([967]) tensor([22.3059],
#       grad_fn=<MaxBackward0>)
```

Using PyTorch's max() function, we see that the class with index 967 has the highest value, 22.3059, and thus is the winner. However, we don't know what class 967 represents. Let's load the file with class names and find out:

```
url = 'https://pytorch.tips/imagenet-labels'

fpath = 'imagenet_class_labels.txt'
urllib.request.urlretrieve(url, fpath)

with open('imagenet_class_labels.txt') as f:
  classes = [line.strip() for line in f.readlines()]

print(classes[967])
# out: 967: 'espresso',
```

Like we did earlier, we use urlretrieve() and download the text file containing descriptions of each class. Then, we read the file using readlines() and create a list containing class names. When we print(classes[967]), it shows us that class 967 is *espresso*!

Using PyTorch's softmax() function, we can convert the output values to probabilities:

```
prob = torch.nn.functional.softmax(y, dim=1)[0] * 100
print(classes[index[0]], prob[index[0]].item())
#967: 'espresso', 87.85208892822266
```

To print the probability at an index, we use PyTorch's tensor.item() method. The item() method is frequently used and returns the numeric value contained in a tensor. The results show that the model is 87.85% sure that this image is an image of an espresso.

We can use PyTorch's `sort()` function to sort the output probabilities and look at the top five:

```
_, indices = torch.sort(y, descending=True)

for idx in indices[0][:5]:
  print(classes[idx], prob[idx].item())
# out:
# 967: 'espresso', 87.85208892822266
# 968: 'cup', 7.28359317779541
# 504: 'coffee mug', 4.33521032333374
# 925: 'consomme', 0.36686763167381287
# 960: 'chocolate sauce, chocolate syrup',
#      0.09037172049283981
```

We see that the model predicts that the image is *espresso* with 87.85% probability. It also predicts *cup* with 7.28% and *coffee mug* with 4.3% probability, but it seems pretty confident that the image is an espresso.

You may feel like you need an espresso right now. We covered a lot in that example! The core code to accomplish everything is actually much shorter. Assuming you have downloaded the files already, you only need to run the following code to classify an image using AlexNet:

```
import torch
from torchvision import transforms, models

transform = transforms.Compose([
  transforms.Resize(256),
  transforms.CenterCrop(224),
  transforms.ToTensor(),
  transforms.Normalize(
      mean=[0.485, 0.456, 0.406],
      std=[0.229, 0.224, 0.225])])

img_tensor = transform(img)
batch = img_tensor.unsqueeze(0)
model = models.alexnet(pretrained=True)

device = "cuda" if torch.cuda.is_available() else "cpu"
model.eval()
model.to(device)
y = model(batch.to(device))

prob = torch.nn.functional.softmax(y, dim=1)[0] * 100
```

```
    _, indices = torch.sort(y, descending=True)
    for idx in indices[0][:5]:
      print(classes[idx], prob[idx].item())
```

And that's how you build an image classifier with PyTorch. Try running your own images through the model and see how it classifies them. Also, try completing the example on another platform. For example, if you used Colab to run the code, try running it locally or in the cloud.

Congratulations, you've verified that your environment is configured properly and that you can execute PyTorch code! We'll explore each topic more deeply throughout the remainder of the book. In the next chapter, we'll explore the fundamentals of PyTorch and provide a quick reference to tensors and their operations.

## CHAPTER 2

Tensors

Before we dive deep into the world of PyTorch development, it's important to familiarize yourself with the fundamental data structure in PyTorch: the torch.Tensor. By understanding the tensor, you will understand how PyTorch handles and stores data, and since deep learning is fundamentally the collection and manipulation of floating-point numbers, understanding tensors will help you understand how PyTorch implements more advanced functions for deep learning. In addition, you may find yourself using tensor operations frequently when pre-processing input data or manipulating output data during model development.

This chapter serves as a quick reference to understanding tensors and implementing tensor functions within your code. I'll begin by describing what a tensor is and show you some simple examples of how to use functions to create, manipulate, and accelerate tensor operations on a GPU. Next, we'll take a broader look at the API for creating tensors and performing math operations so that you can quickly reference a comprehensive list of tensor capabilities. In each section, we will explore some of the more important functions, identify common pitfalls, and examine key points in their usage.

What Is a Tensor?

In PyTorch, a tensor is a data structure used to store and manipulate data. Like a NumPy array, a tensor is a multidimensional array containing elements of a single data type. Tensors can be used to represent scalars, vectors, matrices, and *n*-dimensional arrays and are derived from the torch.Tensor class. However, tensors are more than just arrays of numbers. Creating or instantiating a tensor object from the torch.Tensor class gives us access to a set of built-in class attributes and operations or class methods that provide a robust set of built-in capabilities. This chapter describes these attributes and operations in detail.

Tensors also include added benefits that make them more suitable than NumPy arrays for deep learning calculations. First, tensor operations can be performed significantly faster using GPU acceleration. Second, tensors can be stored and manipulated at scale using distributed processing on multiple CPUs and GPUs and across multiple servers. And third, tensors keep track of their graph computations, which as we will see in "Automatic Differentiation (Autograd)" on page 48 is very important in implementing a deep learning library.

To further explain what a tensor actually is and how to use one, I'll begin by walking through a simple example that creates some tensors and performs a tensor operation.

Simple CPU Example

Here's a simple example that creates a tensor, performs a tensor operation, and uses a built-in method on the tensor itself. By default, the tensor data type will be derived from the input data type and the tensor will be allocated to the CPU device. First, we import the PyTorch library, then we create two tensors, x and y, from two-dimensional lists. Next, we add the two tensors and store the result in z. We can just use the + operator here because the torch.Tensor class supports operator overloading. Finally, we print the new tensor, z, which we can see is the matrix sum of x and y, and we print the size of z. Notice that z is a tensor object itself and the size() method is used to return its matrix dimensions, namely 2×3:

```
import torch

x = torch.tensor([[1,2,3],[4,5,6]])
y = torch.tensor([[7,8,9],[10,11,12]])
z = x + y
print(z)
# out:
# tensor([[ 8, 10, 12],
#         [14, 16, 18]])

print(z.size())
# out: torch.Size([2, 3])
```

NOTE

You may see the torch.Tensor() (capital T) constructor used in legacy code. This is an alias for the default tensor type torch.FloatTensor. You should instead use torch.tensor() to create your tensors.

Simple GPU Example

Since the ability to accelerate tensor operations on a GPU is a major advantage of tensors over NumPy arrays, I'll show you an easy example of this. This is the same example from the last section, but here we move the tensors to the GPU device if one is available. Notice that the output tensor is also allocated to the GPU. You can use the device attribute (e.g., z.device) to double-check where the tensor resides.

In the first line, the torch.cuda.is_available() function will return True if your machine has GPU support. This is a convenient way to write more robust code that can be accelerated when a GPU exists but also runs on a CPU when a GPU is not present. In the output, device='cuda:0' indicates that the first

GPU is being used. If your machine contains multiple GPUs, you can also control which GPU is being used:

```
device = "cuda" if torch.cuda.is_available()
  else "cpu"
x = torch.tensor([[1,2,3],[4,5,6]],
                 device=device)
y = torch.tensor([[7,8,9],[10,11,12]],
                 device=device)
z = x + y
print(z)
# out:
#   tensor([[ 8, 10, 12],
#           [14, 16, 18]], device='cuda:0')

print(z.size())
# out: torch.Size([2, 3])

print(z.device)
# out: cuda:0
```

Moving Tensors Between CPUs and GPUs

The previous code uses torch.tensor() to create a tensor on a specific device; however, it's more common to move an existing tensor to a device, namely a GPU if available. You can do so by using the torch.to() method. When new tensors are created as a result of tensor operations, PyTorch will create the new tensor on the same device. In the following code, z resides on the GPU because x and y reside on the GPU. The tensor z is moved back to the CPU using torch.to("cpu") for further processing. Also note that all the tensors within the operation must be on the same device. If x was on the GPU and y was on the CPU, we would get an error:

```
device = "cuda" if torch.cuda.is_available()
  else "cpu"
x = x.to(device)
y = y.to(device)
z = x + y
z = z.to("cpu")
# out:
# tensor([[ 8, 10, 12],
#         [14, 16, 18]])
```

You can use strings directly as device parameters instead of device objects. The following are all equivalent:

- `device="cuda"`
- `device=torch.device("cuda")`
- `device="cuda:0"`
- `device=torch.device("cuda:0")`

Creating Tensors

The previous section showed a simple way to create tensors; however, there are many other ways to do it. You can create tensors from preexisting numeric data or create random samplings. Tensors can be created from preexisting data stored in array-like structures such as lists, tuples, scalars, or serialized data files, as well as in NumPy arrays.

The following code illustrates some common ways to create tensors. First, it shows how to create a tensor from a list using `torch.tensor()`. This method can also be used to create tensors from other data structures like tuples, sets, or NumPy arrays:

```python
import numpy

# Created from preexisting arrays
w = torch.tensor([1,2,3])          ❶
w = torch.tensor((1,2,3))          ❷
w = torch.tensor(numpy.array([1,2,3]))  ❸

# Initialized by size
w = torch.empty(100,200)           ❹
w = torch.zeros(100,200)           ❺
w = torch.ones(100,200)            ❻
```

❶ From a list

❷ From a tuple

❸ From a NumPy array

❹ Uninitialized; element values are not predictable

❺ All elements initialized with 0.0

❻ All elements initialized with 1.0

As shown in the previous code sample, you can also create and initialize tensors by using functions like `torch.empty()`, `torch.ones()`, and `torch.zeros()` and specifying the desired size.

If you want to initialize a tensor with random values, PyTorch supports a robust set of functions that you can use, such as `torch.rand()`, `torch.randn()`, and `torch.randint()`, as shown in the following code:

```
# Initialized by size with random values
w = torch.rand(100,200)          ❶
w = torch.randn(100,200)         ❷
w = torch.randint(5,10,(100,200)) ❸

# Initialized with specified data type or device
w = torch.empty((100,200), dtype=torch.float64,
                device="cuda")

# Initialized to have the same size, data type,
#   and device as another tensor
x = torch.empty_like(w)
```

❶ Creates a 100 × 200 tensor with elements from a uniform distribution on the interval [0, 1).

❷ Elements are random numbers from a normal distribution with a mean of 0 and a variance of 1.

❸ Elements are random integers between 5 and 10.

Upon initialization, you can specify the data type and device (i.e., CPU or GPU) as shown in the previous code sample. In

---

addition, the example shows how you can use PyTorch to create tensors that have the same properties as other tensors but are initialized with different data. Functions with the _like postfix such as `torch.empty_like()` and `torch.ones_like()` return tensors that have the same size, data type, and device as another tensor but are initialized differently (see "Creating Tensors from Random Samples" on page 32).

NOTE

There are some legacy functions, such as `from_numpy()` and `as_tensor()`, that have been replaced in practice by the `torch.tensor()` constructor, which can be used to handle all cases.

Table 2-1 lists PyTorch functions used to create tensors. You should use each one with the `torch` namespace, e.g., `torch.empty()`. You can find more details by visiting the PyTorch tensor documentation (*https://pytorch.tips/torch*).

Table 2-1. Tensor creation functions

Function	Description
`torch.tensor(data, dtype=None, device=None, requires_grad=False, pin_memory=False)`	Creates a tensor from an existing data structure
`torch.empty(*size, out=None, dtype=None, layout=torch.strided, device=None, requires_grad=False)`	Creates a tensor from uninitialized elements based on the random state of values in memory
`torch.zeros(*size, out=None, dtype=None, layout=torch.strided, device=None, requires_grad=False)`	Creates a tensor with all elements initialized to 0.0

Function	Description
torch.**ones**(*size, out=None, dtype=None, layout=torch.strided, device=None, requires_grad=False)	Creates a tensor with all elements initialized to 1.0
torch.**arange**(start=0, end, step=1, out=None, dtype=None, layout=torch.strided, device=None, requires_grad=False)	Creates a 1D tensor of values over a range with a common step value
torch.**linspace**(start, end, steps=100, out=None, dtype=None, layout=torch.strided, device=None, requires_grad=False)	Creates a 1D tensor of linearly spaced points between the start and end
torch.**logspace**(start, end, steps=100, base=10.0, out=None, dtype=None, layout=torch.strided, device=None, requires_grad=False)	Creates a 1D tensor of logarithmically spaced points between the start and end
torch.**eye**(n, m=None, out=None, dtype=None, layout=torch.strided, device=None, requires_grad=False)	Creates a 2D tensor with ones on the diagonal and zeros everywhere else
torch.**full**(size, fill_value, out=None, dtype=None, layout=torch.strided, device=None, requires_grad=False)	Creates a tensor filled with fill_value
torch.**load**(f)	Loads a tensor from a serialized pickle file
torch.**save**(f)	Saves a tensor to a serialized pickle file

The PyTorch documentation contains a complete list of functions for creating tensors as well as more detailed explanations of how to use them. Here are some common pitfalls and additional insights to keep in mind when creating tensors:

- Most creation functions accept the optional `dtype` and `device` parameters, so you can set these at creation time.

- You should use `torch.arange()` in favor of the deprecated `torch.range()` function. Use `torch.arange()` when the step size is known. Use `torch.linspace()` when the number of elements is known.

- You can use `torch.tensor()` to create tensors from array-like structures such as lists, NumPy arrays, tuples, and sets. To convert existing tensors to NumPy arrays and lists, use the `torch.numpy()` and `torch.tolist()` functions, respectively.

Tensor Attributes

One PyTorch quality that has contributed to its popularity is the fact that it's very Pythonic and object oriented in nature. Since a tensor is its own data type, you can read attributes of the tensor object itself. Now that you can create tensors, it's useful to be able to quickly find information about them by accessing their attributes. Assuming x is a tensor, you can access several attributes of x as follows:

`x.dtype`
> Indicates the tensor's data type (see Table 2-2 for a list of PyTorch data types)

`x.device`
> Indicates the tensor's device location (e.g., CPU or GPU memory)

`x.shape`
> Shows the tensor's dimensions

`x.ndim`
> Identifies the number of a tensor's dimensions or rank

`x.requires_grad`

> A Boolean attribute that indicates whether the tensor keeps track of graph computations (see "Automatic Differentiation (Autograd)" on page 48)

`x.grad`

> Contains the actual gradients if `requires_grad` is `True`

`x.grad_fn`

> Stores the graph computation function used if `requires_grad` is `True`

`x.s_cuda`, `x.is_sparse`, `x.is_quantized`, `x.is_leaf`, `x.is_mkldnn`

> Boolean attributes that indicate whether the tensor meets certain conditions

`x.layout`

> Indicates how a tensor is laid out in memory

Remember that when accessing object attributes, you do not include parentheses (()) like you would with a class method (e.g., use `x.shape`, not `x.shape()`).

Data Types

During deep learning development, it's important to be aware of the data type used by your data and its calculations. So when you create tensors, you should control what data types are being used. As mentioned previously, all tensor elements have the same data type. You can specify the data type when creating the tensor by using the `dtype` parameter, or you can cast a tensor to a new `dtype` using the appropriate casting method or the `to()` method, as shown in the following code:

```
# Specify the data type at creation using dtype
w = torch.tensor([1,2,3], dtype=torch.float32)

# Use the casting method to cast to a new data type
w.int()      # w remains a float32 after the cast
w = w.int()  # w changes to an int32 after the cast

# Use the to() method to cast to a new type
```

```
w = w.to(torch.float64) ❶
w = w.to(dtype=torch.float64) ❷

# Python automatically converts data types during
# operations
x = torch.tensor([1,2,3], dtype=torch.int32)
y = torch.tensor([1,2,3], dtype=torch.float32)
z = x + y ❸
print(z.dtype)
# out: torch.float32
```

❶ Pass in the data type.

❷ Define the data type directly with dtype.

❸ Python automatically converts x to float32 and returns z as float32.

Note that the casting and to() methods do not change the tensor's data type unless you reassign the tensor. Also, when performing operations on mixed data types, PyTorch will automatically cast tensors to the appropriate type.

Most of the tensor creation functions allow you to specify the data type upon creation using the dtype parameter. When you set the dtype or cast tensors, remember to use the torch namespace (e.g., torch.int64, not just int64).

Table 2-2 lists all the available data types in PyTorch. Each data type results in a different tensor class depending on the tensor's device. The corresponding tensor classes are shown in the two rightmost columns for CPUs and GPUs, respectively.

Table 2-2. Tensor data types

Data type	dtype	CPU tensor	GPU tensor
32-bit floating point (default)	torch.float32 or torch.float	torch. FloatTensor	torch.cuda. FloatTensor
64-bit floating point	torch.float64 or torch.double	torch. DoubleTensor	torch.cuda. DoubleTensor

Data type	dtype	CPU tensor	GPU tensor
16-bit floating point	torch.float16 or torch.half	torch. HalfTensor	torch.cuda. HalfTensor
8-bit integer (unsigned)	torch.uint8	torch. ByteTensor	torch.cuda. ByteTensor
8-bit integer (signed)	torch.int8	torch. CharTensor	torch.cuda. CharTensor
16-bit integer (signed)	torch.int16 or torch.short	torch. ShortTensor	torch.cuda. ShortTensor
32-bit integer (signed)	torch.int32 or torch.int	torch. IntTensor	torch.cuda. IntTensor
64-bit integer (signed)	torch.int64 or torch.long	torch. LongTensor	torch.cuda. LongTensor
Boolean	torch.bool	torch. BoolTensor	torch.cuda. BoolTensor

NOTE

To reduce space complexity, you may sometimes want to reuse memory and overwrite tensor values using *in-place operations*. To perform in-place operations, append the underscore (_) postfix to the function name. For example, the function y.add_(x) adds x to y, but the results will be stored in y.

Creating Tensors from Random Samples

The need to create random data comes up often during deep learning development. Sometimes you will need to initialize weights to random values or create random inputs with specified distributions. PyTorch supports a very robust set of functions that you can use to create tensors from random data.

As with other creation functions, you can specify the dtype and device when creating the tensor. Table 2-3 lists some examples of random sampling functions.

Table 2-3. Random sampling functions

Function	Description
torch.**rand**(*size, out=None, dtype=None, layout=torch.strided, device=None, requires_grad=False)	Selects random values from a uniform distribution on the interval [0 to 1]
torch.**randn**(*size, out=None, dtype=None, layout=torch.strided, device=None, requires_grad=False)	Selects random values from a standard normal distribution with zero mean unit variance
torch.**normal**(mean, std, *, generator=None, out=None)	Selects random numbers from a normal distribution with a specified mean and variance
torch.**randint**(low=0, high, size, *, generator=None, out=None, dtype=None, layout=torch.strided, device=None, requires_grad=False)	Selects random integers generated uniformly between specified low and high values
torch.**randperm**(n, out=None, dtype=torch.int64, layout=torch.strided, device=None, requires_grad=False)	Creates a random permutation of integers from 0 to $n-1$
torch.**bernoulli**(input, *, generator=None, out=None)	Draws binary random numbers (0 or 1) from a Bernoulli distribution
torch.**multinomial**(input, num_samples, replacement=False, *, generator=None, out=None)	Selects a random number from a list according to weights from a multinomial distribution

Creating Tensors Like Other Tensors

You may want to create and initialize a tensor that has similar properties to another tensor, including the `dtype`, `device`, and `layout` properties to facilitate calculations. Many of the tensor creation operations have a similarity function that allows you to easily do this. The similarity functions will have the postfix `_like`. For example, `torch.empty_like(tensor_a)` will create an empty tensor with the `dtype`, `device`, and `layout` properties of `tensor_a`. Some examples of similarity functions include `empty_like()`, `zeros_like()`, `ones_like()`, `full_like()`, `rand_like()`, `randn_like()`, and `rand_int_like()`.

Tensor Operations

Now that you understand how to create tensors, let's explore what you can do with them. PyTorch supports a robust set of tensor operations that allow you to access and transform your tensor data.

First I'll describe how to access portions of your data, manipulate their elements, and combine tensors to form new tensors. Then I'll show you how to perform simple calculations as well as advanced mathematical computations, often in constant time. PyTorch provides many built-in functions. It's useful to check what's available before creating your own.

Indexing, Slicing, Combining, and Splitting Tensors

Once you have created tensors, you may want to access portions of the data and combine or split tensors to form new tensors. The following code demonstrates how to perform these types of operations. You can slice and index tensors in the same way you would slice and index NumPy arrays, as shown in the first few lines of the following code. Note that indexing and slicing will return tensors even if the array is only a single element. You will need to use the `item()` function to convert a single-element tensor to a Python value when passing to other functions like `print()`:

```
x = torch.tensor([[1,2],[3,4],[5,6],[7,8]])
print(x)
# out:
# tensor([[1, 2],
#         [3, 4],
#         [5, 6],
#         [7, 8]])

# Indexing, returns a tensor
print(x[1,1])
# out: tensor(4)

# Indexing, returns a value as a Python number
print(x[1,1].item())
# out: 4
```

In the following code, we see that we can perform slicing using the same [*start*:*end*:*step*] format that is used for slicing Python lists and NumPy arrays. We can also use Boolean indexing to extract portions of the data that meet certain criteria, as shown here:

```
# Slicing
print(x[:2,1])
# out: tensor([2, 4])

# Boolean indexing
# Only keep elements less than 5
print(x[x<5])
# out: tensor([1, 2, 3, 4])
```

PyTorch also supports transposing and reshaping arrays, as shown in the next few lines of code:

```
# Transpose array; x.t() or x.T can be used
print(x.t())
# tensor([[1, 3, 5, 7],
#         [2, 4, 6, 8]])

# Change shape; usually view() is preferred over
# reshape()
print(x.view((2,4)))
# tensor([[1, 3, 5, 7],
#         [2, 4, 6, 8]])
```

You can also combine or split tensors by using functions like torch.stack() and torch.unbind(), respectively, as shown in the following code:

```
# Combining tensors
y = torch.stack((x, x))
print(y)
# out:
# tensor([[[1, 2],
#          [3, 4],
#          [5, 6],
#          [7, 8]],

#         [[1, 2],
#          [3, 4],
#          [5, 6],
#          [7, 8]]])

# Splitting tensors
a,b = x.unbind(dim=1)
print(a,b)
# out:
#  tensor([1, 3, 5, 7]); tensor([2, 4, 6, 8])
```

PyTorch provides a robust set of built-in functions that can be used to access, split, and combine tensors in different ways. Table 2-4 lists some commonly used functions to manipulate tensor elements.

Table 2-4. Indexing, slicing, combining, and splitting operations

Function	Description
torch.**cat**()	Concatenates the given sequence of tensors in the given dimension.
torch.**chunk**()	Splits a tensor into a specific number of chunks. Each chunk is a view of the input tensor.
torch.**gather**()	Gathers values along an axis specified by the dimension.
torch.**index_select**()	Returns a new tensor that indexes the input tensor along a dimension using the entries in the index, which is a LongTensor.
torch.**masked_select**()	Returns a new 1D tensor that indexes the input tensor according to the Boolean mask, which is a BoolTensor.
torch.**narrow**()	Returns a tensor that is a narrow version of the input tensor.
torch.**nonzero**()	Returns the indices of nonzero elements.
torch.**reshape**()	Returns a tensor with the same data and number of elements as the input tensor, but a different shape. Use view() instead to ensure the tensor is not copied.
torch.**split**()	Splits the tensor into chunks. Each chunk is a view or subdivision of the original tensor.
torch.**squeeze**()	Returns a tensor with all the dimensions of the input tensor of size 1 removed.
torch.**stack**()	Concatenates a sequence of tensors along a new dimension.
torch.**t**()	Expects the input to be a 2D tensor and transposes dimensions 0 and 1.
torch.**take**()	Returns a tensor at specified indices when slicing is not continuous.
torch.**transpose**()	Transposes only the specified dimensions.

Function	Description
torch.**unbind**()	Removes a tensor dimension by returning a tuple of the removed dimension.
torch.**unsqueeze**()	Returns a new tensor with a dimension of size 1 inserted at the specified position.
torch.**where**()	Returns a tensor of selected elements from either one of two tensors, depending on the specified condition.

Some of these functions may seem redundant. However, the following key distinctions and best practices are important to keep in mind:

- item() is an important and commonly used function to return the Python number from a tensor containing a single value.

- Use view() instead of reshape() for reshaping tensors in most cases. Using reshape() may cause the tensor to be copied, depending on its layout in memory. view() ensures that it will not be copied.

- Using x.T or x.t() is a simple way to transpose 1D or 2D tensors. Use transpose() when dealing with multidimensional tensors.

- The torch.squeeze() function is used often in deep learning to remove an unused dimension. For example, a batch of images with a single image can be reduced from 4D to 3D using squeeze().

- The torch.unsqueeze() function is often used in deep learning to add a dimension of size 1. Since most PyTorch models expect a batch of data as an input, you could apply unsqueeze() when you only have one data sample. For example, you can pass a 3D image into torch.unsqueeze() to create a batch of one image.

Tensor Operations for Mathematics

Deep learning development is strongly based on mathematical computations, so PyTorch supports a very robust set of built-in math functions. Whether you are creating new data transforms, customizing loss functions, or building your own optimization algorithms, you can speed up your research and development with the math functions provided by PyTorch.

The purpose of this section is to provide a quick overview of many of the mathematical functions available in PyTorch so that you can quickly build your awareness of what currently exists and find the appropriate functions when needed.

PyTorch supports many different types of math functions, including pointwise operations, reduction functions, comparison calculations, and linear algebra operations, as well as spectral and other math computations. The first category of useful math operations we'll look at are *pointwise operations*. Pointwise operations perform an operation on each point in the tensor individually and return a new tensor.

They are useful for rounding and truncation as well as trigonometrical and logical operations. By default, the functions will create a new tensor or use one passed in by the out parameter. If you want to perform an in-place operation, remember to append an underscore to the function name.

Table 2-5 lists some commonly used pointwise operations.

Table 2-5. Pointwise operations

Operation type	Sample functions
Basic math	add(), div(), mul(), neg(), reciprocal(), true_divide()
Truncation	ceil(), clamp(), floor(), floor_divide(), fmod(), frac(), lerp(), remainder(), round(), sigmoid(), trunc()
Complex numbers	abs(), angle(), conj(), imag(), real()
Trigonometry	acos(), asin(), atan(), cos(), cosh(), deg2rad(), rad2deg(), sin(), sinh(), tan(), tanh()
Exponents and logarithms	exp(), expm1(), log(), log10(), log1p(), log2(), logaddexp(), pow(), rsqrt(), sqrt(), square()
Logical	logical_and(), logical_not(), logical_or(), logical_xor()
Cumulative math	addcdiv(), addcmul()
Bitwise operators	bitwise_not(), bitwise_and(), bitwise_or(), bitwise_xor()
Error functions	erf(), erfc(), erfinv()
Gamma functions	digamma(), lgamma(), mvlgamma(), polygamma()

Use Python hints or refer to the PyTorch documentation for details on function usage. Note that true_divide() converts tensor data to floats first and should be used when dividing integers to obtain true division results.

The second category of math functions we'll look at are *reduction operations*. Reduction operations reduce a bunch of numbers down to a single number or a smaller set of numbers. That is, they reduce the *dimensionality* or *rank* of the tensor. Reduction operations include functions for finding maximum or minimum values as well as many statistical calculations, like finding the mean or standard deviation.

These operations are frequently used in deep learning. For example, deep learning classification often uses the argmax() function to reduce softmax outputs to a dominant class.

Table 2-6 lists some commonly used reduction operations.

Table 2-6. Reduction operations

Function	Description
torch.**argmax**(*input, dim, keepdim=False, out=None*)	Returns the index(es) of the maximum value across all elements, or just a dimension if it's specified
torch.**argmin**(*input, dim, keepdim=False, out=None*)	Returns the index(es) of the minimum value across all elements, or just a dimension if it's specified
torch.**dist**(*input, dim, keepdim=False, out=None*)	Computes the p-norm of two tensors

Function	Description
torch.**logsumexp**(*input, dim, keepdim=False, out=None*)	Computes the log of summed exponentials of each row of the input tensor in the given dimension
torch.**mean**(*input, dim, keepdim=False, out=None*)	Computes the mean or average across all elements, or just a dimension if it's specified
torch.**median**(*input, dim, keepdim=False, out=None*)	Computes the median or middle value across all elements, or just a dimension if it's specified
torch.**mode**(*input, dim, keepdim=False, out=None*)	Computes the mode or most frequent value across all elements, or just a dimension if it's specified
torch.**norm**(*input, p='fro', dim=None, keepdim=False, out=None, dtype=None*)	Computes the matrix or vector norm across all elements, or just a dimension if it's specified
torch.**prod**(*input, dim, keepdim=False, dtype=None*)	Computes the product of all elements, or of each row of the input tensor if it's specified
torch.**std**(*input, dim, keepdim=False, out=None*)	Computes the standard deviation across all elements, or just a dimension if it's specified
torch.**std_mean**(*input, unbiased=True*)	Computes the standard deviation and mean across all elements, or just a dimension if it's specified
torch.**sum**(*input, dim, keepdim=False, out=None*)	Computes the sum of all elements, or just a dimension if it's specified
torch.**unique**(*input, dim, keepdim=False, out=None*)	Removes duplicates across the entire tensor, or just a dimension if it's specified
torch.**unique_consecutive**(*input, dim, keepdim=False, out=None*)	Similar to torch.unique() but only removes consecutive duplicates

Function	Description
torch.**var**(*input, dim, keepdim=False, out=None*)	Computes the variance across all elements, or just a dimension if it's specified
torch.**var_mean**(*input, dim, keepdim=False, out=None*)	Computes the mean and variance across all elements, or just a dimension if it's specified

Note that many of these functions accept the dim parameter, which specifies the dimension of reduction for multidimensional tensors. This is similar to the axis parameter in NumPy. By default, when dim is not specified, the reduction occurs across all dimensions. Specifying dim = 1 will compute the operation across each row. For example, torch.mean(x,1) will compute the mean for each row in tensor x.

TIP

It's common to chain methods together. For example, torch.rand(2,2).max().item() creates a 2 × 2 tensor of random floats, finds the maximum value, and returns the value itself from the resulting tensor.

Next, we'll look at PyTorch's *comparison functions*. Comparison functions usually compare all the values within a tensor, or compare one tensor's values to another's. They can return a tensor full of Booleans based on each element's value such as torch.eq() or torch.is_boolean(). There are also functions to find the maximum or minimum value, sort tensor values, return the top subset of tensor elements, and more.

Table 2-7 lists some commonly used comparison functions for your reference.

Table 2-7. Comparison operations

Operation type	Sample functions
Compare a tensor to other tensors	`eq()`, `ge()`, `gt()`, `le()`, `lt()`, `ne()` or `==`, `>`, `>=`, `<`, `<=`, `!=`, respectively
Test tensor status or conditions	`isclose()`, `isfinite()`, `isinf()`, `isnan()`
Return a single Boolean for the entire tensor	`allclose()`, `equal()`
Find value(s) over the entire tensor or along a given dimension	`argsort()`, `kthvalue()`, `max()`, `min()`, `sort()`, `topk()`,

Comparison functions seem pretty straightforward; however, there are a few key points to keep in mind. Common pitfalls include the following:

- The `torch.eq()` function or `==` returns a tensor of the same size with a Boolean result for each element. The `torch.equal()` function tests if the tensors are the same size, and if all elements within the tensor are equal then it returns a single Boolean value.

- The function `torch.allclose()` also returns a single Boolean value if all elements are close to a specified value.

The next type of mathematical functions we'll look at are *linear algebra functions*. Linear algebra functions facilitate matrix operations and are important for deep learning computations.

Many computations, including gradient descent and optimization algorithms, use linear algebra to implement their calculations. PyTorch supports a robust set of built-in linear algebra operations, many of which are based on the Basic Linear Algebra Subprograms (BLAS) and Linear Algebra Package (LAPACK) standardized libraries.

Table 2-8 lists some commonly used linear algebra operations.

Table 2-8. Linear algebra operations

Function	Description
torch.matmul()	Computes a matrix product of two tensors; supports broadcasting
torch.chain_matmul()	Computes a matrix product of *N* tensors
torch.mm()	Computes a matrix product of two tensors (if broadcasting is required, use matmul())
torch.addmm()	Computes a matrix product of two tensors and adds it to the input
torch.bmm()	Computes a batch of matrix products
torch.addbmm()	Computes a batch of matrix products and adds it to the input
torch.baddbmm()	Computes a batch of matrix products and adds it to the input batch
torch.mv()	Computes the product of the matrix and vector
torch.addmv()	Computes the product of the matrix and vector and adds it to the input
torch.matrix_power	Returns a tensor raised to the power of *n* (for square tensors)
torch.eig()	Finds the eigenvalues and eigenvectors of a real square tensor
torch.inverse()	Computes the inverse of a square tensor
torch.det()	Computes the determinant of a matrix or batch of matrices
torch.logdet()	Computes the log determinant of a matrix or batch of matrices
torch.dot()	Computes the inner product of two tensors
torch.addr()	Computes the outer product of two tensors and adds it to the input

Function	Description
torch.**solve**()	Returns the solution to a system of linear equations
torch.**svd**()	Performs a single-value decomposition
torch.**pca_low rank**()	Performs a linear principle component analysis
torch.**cholesky**()	Computes a Cholesky decomposition
torch.**cho lesky_inverse**()	Computes the inverse of a symmetric positive definite matrix and returns the Cholesky factor
torch.**cho lesky_solve**()	Solves a system of linear equations using the Cholesky factor

The functions in Table 2-8 range from matrix multiplication and batch calculations functions to solvers. It's important to point out that matrix multiplication is not the same as pointwise multiplication with torch.mul() or the * operator.

A complete study of linear algebra is beyond the scope of this book, but you may find it useful to access some of the linear algebra functions when performing feature reduction or developing custom deep learning algorithms. See the PyTorch linear algebra documentation (*https://pytorch.tips/linear-algebra*) for a complete list of available functions and more details on how to use them.

The final type of mathematical operations we'll consider are *spectral and other math operations*. Depending on the domain of interest, these functions may be useful for data transforms or analysis. For example, spectral operations like the fast Fourier transform (FFT) can play an important role in computer vision or digital signal processing applications.

Table 2-9 lists some built-in operations for spectrum analysis and other mathematical operations.

Table 2-9. Spectral and other math operations

Operation type	Sample functions
Fast, inverse, and short-time Fourier transforms	`fft()`, `ifft()`, `stft()`
Real-to-complex FFT and complex-to-real inverse FFT (IFFT)	`rfft()`, `irfft()`
Windowing algorithms	`bartlett_window()`, `blackman_window()`, `hamming_window()`, `hann_window()`
Histogram and bin counts	`histc()`, `bincount()`
Cumulative operations	`cummax()`, `cummin()`, `cumprod()`, `cumsum()`, `trace()` (sum of the diagonal), `einsum()` (sum of products using Einstein summation)
Normalization functions	`cdist()`, `renorm()`
Cross product, dot product, and Cartesian product	`cross()`, `tensordot()`, `cartesian_prod()`
Functions that create a diagonal tensor with elements of the input tensor	`diag()`, `diag_embed()`, `diag_flat()`, `diagonal()`
Einstein summation	`einsum()`
Matrix reduction and restructuring functions	`flatten()`, `flip()`, `rot90()`, `repeat_interleave()`, `meshgrid()`, `roll()`, `combinations()`
Functions that return the lower or upper triangles and their indices	`tril()`, `tril_indices`, `triu()`, `triu_indices()`

Automatic Differentiation (Autograd)

One function, `backward()`, is worth calling out in its own sub-section because it's what makes PyTorch so powerful for deep learning development. The `backward()` function uses PyTorch's automatic differentiation package, `torch.autograd`, to differentiate and compute gradients of tensors based on the chain rule.

Here's a simple example of autodifferentiation. We define a function, $f = \text{sum}(x^2)$, where x is a matrix of variables. If we want to find df / dx for each variable in the matrix, we need to set the `requires_grad = True` flag for the tensor x, as shown in the following code:

```
x = torch.tensor([[1,2,3],[4,5,6]],
        dtype=torch.float, requires_grad=True)
print(x)
# out:
# tensor([[1., 2., 3.],
#         [4., 5., 6.]], requires_grad=True)

f = x.pow(2).sum()
print(f)
# tensor(91., grad_fn=<SumBackward0>)

f.backward()
print(x.grad) # df/dx = 2x
# tensor([[ 2.,  4.,  6.],
#         [ 8., 10., 12.]])
```

The `f.backward()` function performs the differentiation with respect to f and stores df / dx in the `x.grad` attribute. A quick review of calculus differential equations will tell us the derivation of f with respect to x, $df / dx = 2x$. The results of evaluating df / dx for the values of x are shown as the output.

NOTE

Only tensors of floating-point `dtype` can require gradients.

Training NNs requires us to compute the weight gradients on the backward pass. As our NNs get deeper and more complex, this feature automates the complex computations. For more information on how autograd works, see the Autograd tutorial (*https://pytorch.tips/autograd-explained*).

This chapter provided a quick reference for creating tensors and performing operations. Now that you have a good foundation on tensors, we will focus on how to use tensors and PyTorch to perform deep learning research. In the next chapter, we will review the deep learning development process before jumping into writing code.

## CHAPTER 3

Deep Learning Development with PyTorch

Now that you have your development environment running and a good understanding of tensors and their operations, we can start developing and deploying deep learning models with PyTorch. This chapter provides a quick reference to the basic NN development process and the PyTorch code needed to execute it.

First we'll review the overall process, then we'll dive into each stage and look at some sample PyTorch code that implements each function. We'll build off what you learned in Chapter 2 to load your data into tensors and apply data transforms that convert your tensors to suitable inputs for your model.

You'll build a deep learning model and train the model using a common training loop structure. Then, you'll test your model's performance and tweak hyperparameters to improve your results and training speed. Finally, we'll explore ways to deploy your model to prototype systems or production. At each stage, I'll provide commonly used PyTorch code for you to use as a reference as you develop your own deep learning models.

Future chapters in this book will provide additional examples and cover more advanced topics, such as customization, optimization, acceleration, distributed training, and advanced deployment. For now, we'll focus on the basic NN development process.

The Overall Process

Although everyone builds their deep learning models in a different way, the overall process is pretty much the same. Regardless of whether you are conducting supervised learning with labeled data, unsupervised learning with unlabeled data, or semisupervised learning with a mixture of both, a basic pipeline is used to train, test, and deploy your deep learning models. I will assume that you have some familiarity with deep learning model development, but before we get started, let's review the basic deep learning training process. Then I'll show how you can implement this process in PyTorch.

Figure 3-1 illustrates the most common tasks in deep learning development. The first stage is the data preparation stage, in which we will load data from an external source and convert it to the appropriate format for model training. This data could be images, videos, speech recordings, audio files, text, general tabular data, or any combination of these.

First, we load this data and convert it to numeric values in the form of tensors. The tensors will act as inputs during the model training stage; however, before they are passed in, the tensors are usually preprocessed via transforms and grouped into batches for better training performance. Thus, the data preparation stage takes generic data and converts it to batches of tensors that can be passed into your NN model.

Next, in the model experimentation and development stage, we will design an NN model, train the model with our training data, test its performance, and optimize our hyperparameters to improve performance to a desired level. To do so, we will separate our dataset into three parts: one for training, one for validation, and one for testing. We'll design an NN model and train its parameters with our training data. PyTorch provides elegantly designed modules and classes in the torch.nn module to help you create and train your NNs. We will define a loss function and optimizer from a selection of the many built-in PyTorch functions. Then we'll perform backpropagation and update the model parameters in our training loop.

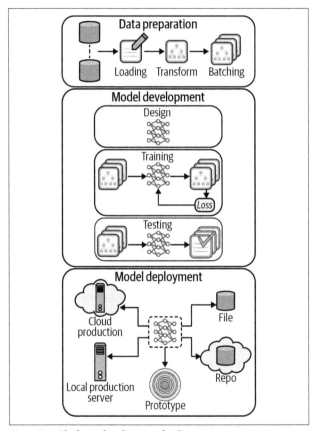

Figure 3-1. The basic deep learning development process

Within each epoch, we'll also validate our model by passing in validation data, measuring performance, and potentially tuning hyperparameters. Finally, we'll test our model by passing in test data and measuring the model's performance against unseen data. In practice, validation and test loops may be optional, but we show them here for completeness.

The last stage of deep learning model development is the model deployment stage. In this stage, we have a fully trained model— so what do we do with it? If you are a deep learning research scientist conducting experiments, you may want to simply save the model to a file and load it for further research and experimentation, or you may want to provide access to it via a repository like PyTorch Hub. You may also want to deploy it to an edge device or local server to demonstrate a prototype or a proof of concept.

On the other hand, if you are a software developer or systems engineer, you may want to deploy your model to a product or service. In this case, you can deploy your model to a production environment on a cloud server or deploy it to an edge device or mobile phone. When deploying trained models, the model often requires additional postprocessing. For example, you may classify a batch of images, but you only want to report the most confident result. The model deployment stage also handles any postprocessing that is needed to go from your model's output values to the final solution.

Now that we've explored the overall development process, let's dive into each part and show how PyTorch can help you develop deep learning models.

Data Preparation

The first stage of deep learning development starts with data preparation. In this stage, we acquire data to train and test our NN models and convert it to a tensor of numbers that our PyTorch models can process. The size of the dataset and the data itself are important to developing good models; however, generating good datasets is beyond the scope of this book.

In this section, I'll assume that you've already determined the data is good, so I'll focus on describing how to load the data, apply transforms, and batch the data using PyTorch's built-in capabilities. First I'll show how you can prepare image data with the torchvision package, then we'll explore PyTorch resources for preparing other types of data.

Data Loading

PyTorch provides powerful built-in classes and utilities, such as the Dataset, DataLoader, and Sampler classes, for loading various types of data. The Dataset class defines how to access and preprocess data from a file or data sources. The Sampler class defines how to sample data from a dataset in order to create batches, while the DataLoader class combines a dataset with a sampler and allows you to iterate over a set of batches.

PyTorch libraries such as Torchvision and Torchtext also provide classes to support specialized data like computer vision and natural language data. The torchvision.datasets module is a good example of how to utilize built-in classes to load data. The torchvision.datasets module provides a number of subclasses to load image data from popular academic datasets.

One of these popular datasets is CIFAR-10. The CIFAR-10 dataset was collected by Alex Krizhevsky, Vinod Nair, and Geoffrey Hinton during their research for the Canadian Institute for Advanced Research (CIFAR). It consists of 50,000 training images and 10,000 test images of 10 possible objects: airplanes, cars, birds, cats, deer, dogs, frogs, horses, ships, and trucks. The following code shows how to use CIFAR-10 to create a training dataset:

```
from torchvision.datasets import CIFAR10

train_data = CIFAR10(root="./train/",
                     train=True,
                     download=True)
```

The `train` parameter determines whether we load the training data or the testing data, and setting `download` to `True` will download the data for us if we don't have it already.

Let's explore the `train_data` dataset object. We can access information about the dataset using its methods and attributes as shown in the following code:

```
print(train_data) ❶
# out:
# Dataset CIFAR10
#     Number of datapoints: 50000
#     Root location: ./train/
#     Split: Train

print(len(train_data)) ❷
# out: 50000

print(train_data.data.shape) # ndarray ❸
# out: (50000, 32, 32, 3)

print(train_data.targets) # list ❹
# out: [6, 9, ...,  1, 1]

print(train_data.classes) ❺
# out: ['airplane', 'automobile', 'bird',
#       'cat', 'deer', 'dog', 'frog',
#       'horse', 'ship', 'truck']

print(train_data.class_to_idx) ❻
# out:
# {'airplane': 0, 'automobile': 1, 'bird': 2,
#  'cat': 3, 'deer': 4, 'dog': 5, 'frog': 6,
#  'horse': 7, 'ship': 8, 'truck': 9}
```

❶ Printing the object returns its general information.

❷ Check the number of data samples with `len()`.

❸ The data is a NumPy array of 50,000 32 × 32-pixel color images.

❹ The targets are a list of 50,000 data labels.

❺ You can map numeric labels to class names using `classes`.

❻ You can map class names to index values using `class_to_idx`.

Let's take a closer look at the `train_data` dataset's data and labels. We can access a data sample using an index, as shown in the following code:

```
print(type(train_data[0]))
# out: <class 'tuple'>

print(len(train_data[0]))
# out: 2

data, label = train_data[0]
```

As you can see in the code, `train_data[0]` returns a tuple with two elements—the data and the label. Let's examine the data first:

```
print(type(data))
# out: <class 'PIL.Image.Image'>

print(data)
# out:
# <PIL.Image.Image image mode=RGB
#        size=32x32 at 0x7FA61-D6F1748>
```

The data consists of a PIL image object. PIL is a common image format that uses the Pillow library to store image pixel values in the format of height × width × channels. A color image has three channels (RGB) for red, green, and blue. The data format is good to know because we may need to convert this format for our model if the model expects a different format (more on this later).

Figure 3-2 shows the PIL image. It's a little blurry because the resolution is only 32 × 32, but can you tell what it is?

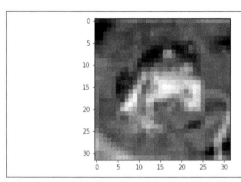

Figure 3-2. Sample image

Let's examine the label:

```
print(type(label))
# out: <class 'int'>

print(label)
# out: 6

print(train_data.classes[label])
# out: frog
```

In the code, the `label` is an integer value representing the class of the image (e.g., airplane, dog, etc.). We can use the `classes` attribute to see that an index of 6 corresponds to a frog.

We can also load the test data into another dataset object called `test_data`. Changing the root folder and setting the `train` flag to `False` will do the trick, as shown in the following code:

```
test_data = CIFAR10(root="./test/",
                    train=False,
                    download=True)

print(test_data)
# out:
# Dataset CIFAR10
#     Number of datapoints: 10000
#     Root location: ./test/
#     Split: Test

print(len(test_data))
```

```
# out: 10000

print(test_data.data.shape) # ndarray
# out: (10000, 32, 32, 3)
```

The `test_data` dataset is similar to the `train_data` dataset. However, there are only 10,000 images in the test dataset. Try accessing some of the methods from the dataset class and the attributes on the `test_data` dataset yourself.

Data Transforms

In the data loading step, we pulled data from its source and created dataset objects that contain information about the dataset and the data itself. However, the data might need to be adjusted before it is passed into the NN model for training and testing. For example, data values may be normalized to assist training, augmented to create larger datasets, or converted from one type of object to a tensor.

These adjustments are accomplished by applying *transforms*. The beauty of using transforms in PyTorch is that you can define a sequence of transforms and apply it when the data is accessed. Later, in Chapter 5, you'll see how you can even apply transforms on a CPU in parallel with your training on a GPU.

In the following code example, we'll define our transforms and create our `train_data` dataset using these transforms:

```
from torchvision import transforms

train_transforms = transforms.Compose([
  transforms.RandomCrop(32, padding=4),
  transforms.RandomHorizontalFlip(),
  transforms.ToTensor(),
  transforms.Normalize(
      mean=(0.4914, 0.4822, 0.4465),      ❶
      std=(0.2023, 0.1994, 0.2010))])

train_data = CIFAR10(root="./train/",
                     train=True,
                     download=True,
                     transform=train_transforms)      ❷
```

❶ The mean and standard deviation values here were predetermined based on the dataset itself.

❷ Set the `transform` parameter when creating the dataset.

We define a set of transforms using the `transforms.Compose()` class. This class accepts a list of transforms and applies them in sequence. Here we randomly crop and flip images, convert them to tensors, and normalize the tensor values to predetermined means and standard deviations.

The transforms are passed to the dataset class during instantiation and become part of the dataset object. The transforms are applied whenever the dataset object is accessed, returning a new result consisting of the transformed data.

We can view the transforms by printing the dataset or its `transforms` attribute, as shown in the following code:

```
print(train_data)
# out:
# Dataset CIFAR10
#     Number of datapoints: 50000
#     Root location: ./train/
#     Split: Train
#     StandardTransform
# Transform: Compose(
#                 RandomCrop(size=(32, 32),
#                   padding=4)
#                 RandomHorizontalFlip(p=0.5)
#                 ToTensor()
#                 Normalize(
#                   mean=(0.4914, 0.4822, 0.4465),
#                   std=(0.2023, 0.1994, 0.201))
#             )

print(train_data.transforms)
# out:
# StandardTransform
# Transform: Compose(
#                 RandomCrop(size=(32, 32),
#                   padding=4)
#                 RandomHorizontalFlip(p=0.5)
#                 ToTensor()
#                 Normalize(
```

```
#                    mean=(0.4914, 0.4822, 0.4465),
#                    std=(0.2023, 0.1994, 0.201))
```

We can access the data using indexing, as shown in the next code block. PyTorch automatically applies the transforms when the data is accessed, so the output data will be different from what we saw earlier:

```
data, label = train_data[0]

print(type(data))
# out: <class 'torch.Tensor'>

print(data.size())
# out: torch.Size([3, 32, 32])

print(data)
# out:
# tensor([[[-0.1416,  ..., -2.4291],
#          [-0.0060,  ..., -2.4291],
#          [-0.7426,  ..., -2.4291],
#          ...,
#          [ 0.5100,  ..., -2.2214],
#          [-2.2214,  ..., -2.2214],
#          [-2.2214,  ..., -2.2214]]])
```

As you can see, the data output is now a tensor of size $3 \times 32 \times 32$. It has also been randomly cropped, horizontally flipped, and normalized. Figure 3-3 shows the image after applying the transforms.

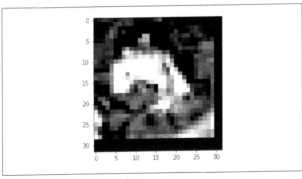

Figure 3-3. Image after transforms

The colors may look strange because of the normalization, but this actually helps NN models do a better job of classifying the images.

We can define a different set of transforms for testing and apply them to our test data as well. In the case of test data, we do not want to crop or flip the image, but we do need to convert the image to tensors and normalize the tensor values, as shown in the following code:

```
test_transforms = transforms.Compose([
  transforms.ToTensor(),
  transforms.Normalize(
      (0.4914, 0.4822, 0.4465),
      (0.2023, 0.1994, 0.2010))])

test_data = torchvision.datasets.CIFAR10(
      root="./test/",
      train=False,
      transform=test_transforms)

print(test_data)
# out:
# Dataset CIFAR10
#     Number of datapoints: 10000
#     Root location: ./test/
#     Split: Test
#     StandardTransform
# Transform: Compose(
#     ToTensor()
#     Normalize(
#       mean=(0.4914, 0.4822, 0.4465),
#       std=(0.2023, 0.1994, 0.201)))
```

Data Batching

Now that we have defined the transforms and created the datasets, we can access data samples one at a time. However, when you train your model, you will want to pass in small batches of data at each iteration, as we will see in "Model Development" on page 68. Sending data in batches not only allows more efficient training but also takes advantage of the parallel nature of GPUs to accelerate training.

Batch processing can easily be implemented using the `torch.utils.data.DataLoader` class. Let's start with an example of how Torchvision uses this class, and then we'll cover it in more detail.

In the following code, we create a dataloader for `train_data` that we can use to load a batch of samples and apply our transforms:

```
trainloader = torch.utils.data.DataLoader(
                    train_data,
                    batch_size=16,
                    shuffle=True)
```

We use a batch size of 16 samples and shuffle our dataset so that the dataloader retrieves a random sampling of the data.

The dataloader object combines a dataset and a sampler, and provides an iterable over the given dataset. In other words, your training loop can use this object to sample your dataset and apply transforms one batch at a time instead of applying them for the complete dataset at once. This considerably improves efficiency and speed when training and testing models.

The following code shows how to retrieve a batch of samples from the `trainloader`:

```
data_batch, labels_batch = next(iter(trainloader))
print(data_batch.size())
# out: torch.Size([16, 3, 32, 32])

print(labels_batch.size())
# out: torch.Size([16])
```

We need to use `iter()` to cast the `trainloader` to an iterator and then use `next()` to iterate over the data one more time. This is only necessary when accessing one batch. As we'll see later, our training loops will access the dataloader directly without the need for `iter()` and `next()`. After checking the sizes of the data and labels, we see they return batches of size 16.

We can create a dataloader for our `test_data` dataset as shown in the following code:

```
testloader = torch.utils.data.DataLoader(
                    test_data,
                    batch_size=16,
                    shuffle=False)
```

Here, we set `shuffle` to `False` since there's usually no need to shuffle the test data and researchers like to see repeatable test results.

General Data Preparation (torch.utils.data)

So far, I've shown you how to load, transform, and batch image data using Torchvision. However, you can use PyTorch to prepare other types of data as well. PyTorch libraries such as Torchtext and Torchaudio provide dataset and dataloader classes for text and audio data, and new external libraries are being developed all the time.

PyTorch also provides a submodule called `torch.utils.data` that you can use to create your own dataset and dataloader classes like the ones you saw in Torchvision. It consists of `Dataset`, `Sampler`, and `DataLoader` classes.

Dataset classes

PyTorch supports map- and iterable-style dataset classes. A *map-style dataset* is derived from the abstract class `torch.utils.data.Dataset`. It implements the `getitem()` and `len()` functions, and represents a map from (possibly nonintegral) indices/keys to data samples. For example, such a dataset, when accessed with `dataset[idx]`, could read the idx-th image and its corresponding label from a folder on the disk. Map-style datasets are more commonly used than iterable-style datasets, and all datasets that represent a map made from keys or data samples should use this subclass.

All subclasses should overwrite `getitem()`, which fetches a data sample for a given key. Subclasses can also optionally overwrite `len()`, which returns the size of the dataset by many `Sampler` implementations and the default options of `DataLoader`.

An *iterable-style dataset*, on the other hand, is derived from the `torch.utils.data.IterableDataset` abstract class. It implements the `iter()` protocol and represents an iterable over data samples. This type of dataset is typically used when reading data from a database or a remote server, as well as data generated in real time. Iterable datasets are useful when random reads are expensive or uncertain, and when the batch size depends on fetched data.

PyTorch's `torch.utils.data` submodule also provides dataset operations to convert, combine, or split dataset objects. These operations include the following:

`TensorDataset(tensors)`
    Creates a dataset object from a tensor

`ConcatDataset(datasets)`
    Creates a dataset from multiple datasets

`ChainDataset(datasets)`
    Chains multiple `IterableDatasets`

`Subset(dataset, indices)`
    Creates a subset of a dataset from specified indices

Sampler classes

In addition to dataset classes PyTorch also provides sampler classes, which offer a way to iterate over indices of dataset samples. Sampler are derived from the `torch.utils.data.Sampler` base class.

Every `Sampler` subclass needs to implement an `iter()` method to provide a way to iterate over indices of dataset elements and a `len()` method that returns the length of the returned iterators. Table 3-1 provides a list of available samplers for your reference.

Table 3-1. Dataset samplers (`torch.utils.data`)

Sampler	Description
`SequentialSampler(data_source)`	Samples data in sequence
`RandomSampler(data_source, replacement=False, num_samples=None, generator=None)`	Samples data randomly
`SubsetRandomSampler(indices, generator=None)`	Samples data randomly from a subset of the dataset
`WeightedRandomSampler(weights, num_samples, replacement=True, generator=None)`	Samples randomly from a weighted distribution
`BatchSampler(sampler, batch_size, drop_last)`	Returns a batch of samples
`distributed.DistributedSampler(dataset, num_replicas=None, rank=None, shuffle=True, seed=0)`	Samples across distributed datasets

Samplers are usually not used directly. They are often passed to dataloaders to define the way the dataloader samples the dataset.

DataLoader classes

The `Dataset` class returns a dataset object that includes data and information about the data. The `Sampler` class returns the actual data itself in a specified or random fashion. The `Data Loader` class combines a dataset with a sampler and returns an iterable.

The dataset and sampler objects are not iterables, meaning you cannot run a `for` loop on them. The dataloader object solves this problem. We used the `DataLoader` class to construct a dataloader object for our CIFAR-10 example earlier in this chapter. The `DataLoader` prototype is shown in the following code:

```
torch.utils.data.DataLoader(
                dataset,
                batch_size=1,
                shuffle=False,
                sampler=None,
                batch_sampler=None,
                num_workers=0,
                collate_fn=None,
                pin_memory=False,
                drop_last=False,
                timeout=0,
                worker_init_fn=None,
                multiprocessing_context=None,
                generator=None)
```

The `dataset`, `batch_size`, `shuffle`, and `sampler` parameters are the most commonly used. The `num_workers` parameter is often used to increase the number of CPU processes that generate batches in parallel. The rest of the parameters are used only for advanced cases.

If you write your own dataset class, all you need to do is call the built-in `DataLoader` to generate an iterable for your data. There is no need to create a dataloader class from scratch.

This section provided a quick reference to the data preparation capabilities of PyTorch. Now that you understand how you can load, transform, and batch your data with PyTorch, you can begin to use your data to develop and train deep learning.

Model Development

Most research and development is focused on developing new and innovative deep learning models. The model development process consists of several steps. At this point, I assume that you have created good datasets and have prepared them for processing by your model.

The first step in the process is model design, in which you design one or more model architectures and initialize the model's parameters (e.g., weights and biases.) It's common practice to start with an existing design and then modify it or create your own. I'll show you how to do both in this section.

The next step is training. During training you'll pass training data through your model, measure the error or loss, and adjust the parameters to improve the results.

During validation, you'll measure the performance of your model against validation data that was not used during training. This helps to guard against *overfitting*, where the model performs well against training data but does not generalize to other input data.

Finally, the model development process often concludes with testing. Testing is when you measure the performance of your trained model against previously unseen data. This section provides a quick reference on how to accomplish the steps and substeps of model development in PyTorch.

Model Design

Model design research has expanded significantly over the past decade, in all industries and fields. Thousands of papers are written every year in areas like computer vision, natural language processing, speech recognition, and audio processing to solve problems such as early cancer detection and innovate new technologies such as self-driving cars. As a result, there are many different types of model architectures to choose from,

---

depending on the problem you're trying to solve. You may even create some of your own!

Using existing and pretrained models

Most users begin model development by selecting an existing model. Maybe you would like to start off with an existing design and make minor modifications or experiment with small improvements before designing your own architecture. You can also use models or parts of an existing model that have already been trained with tons of data.

PyTorch provides many resources to leverage existing model designs and pretrained NNs. One example resource is the PyTorch-based torchvision library for computer vision. The torchvision.models subpackage contains definitions of models for addressing different tasks, including image classification, pixelwise semantic segmentation, object detection, instance segmentation, person keypoint detection, and video classification.

Let's say we want to use the famous VGG16 model for our design. VGG16 (also called OxfordNet) is a convolutional NN architecture named after the Visual Geometry Group from Oxford, who developed it. It was submitted to the Large Scale Visual Recognition Challenge in 2014 and achieved 92.7% top-5 test accuracy on ImageNet, a very large dataset of 14 million hand-annotated images.

We can easily create a pretrained VGG16 model as shown in the following code:

```
from torchvision import models

vgg16 = models.vgg16(pretrained=True)
```

By default, the model will be untrained and have randomly initialized weights. However, in our situation we want to use a pretrained model, so we set pretrained = True. This downloads the weights that were pretrained with the ImageNet dataset and initializes our model's weights with these values.

You can view the sequence of layers contained in the VGG16 model by printing the model. The VGG16 model consists of three parts: features, avgpool, and classifier. It's too large to print all the layers here, so we'll just print the classifier part:

```
print(vgg16.classifier)

# out:
# Sequential(
#   (0): Linear(in_features=25088,
#               out_features=4096, bias=True)
#   (1): ReLU(inplace=True)
#   (2): Dropout(p=0.5, inplace=False)
#   (3): Linear(in_features=4096,
#               out_features=4096, bias=True)
#   (4): ReLU(inplace=True)
#   (5): Dropout(p=0.5, inplace=False)
#   (6): Linear(in_features=4096,
#               out_features=1000, bias=True)
# )
```

Linear, ReLU, and Dropout are torch.nn modules. torch.nn is used to create NN layers, activations, loss functions, and other NN components. Don't worry about it too much right now; we'll cover it in more detail in the next section.

There are many famous untrained and pretrained models available, including AlexNet, VGG, ResNet, Inception, and Mobile-Net, to name a few. Refer to the Torchvision model documentation (*https://pytorch.tips/torchvision-models*) for a complete list of models and details regarding their use.

PyTorch Hub is another excellent resource for existing and pretrained PyTorch models. You can load models from another repository using the torch.hub.load() API. The following code shows how you would load a model from PyTorch Hub:

```
waveglow = torch.hub.load(
    'nvidia/DeepLearningExamples:torchhub',
    'nvidia_waveglow')
```

Here we load a model called WaveGlow that is used to generate speech from the NVIDIA DeepLearningExamples repository.

You can find a list of PyTorch Hub repositories at the main PyTorch Hub site. (*https://pytorch.tips/pytorch-hub*) To explore all the available API endpoints of a particular repository you can use the `torch.hub.list()` function on the repository, as shown in the following code:

```
torch.hub.list(
        'nvidia/DeepLearningExamples:torchhub')

# out:
# ['checkpoint_from_distributed',
#  'nvidia_ncf',
#  'nvidia_ssd',
#  'nvidia_ssd_processing_utils',
#  'nvidia_tacotron2',
#  'nvidia_waveglow',
#  'unwrap_distributed']
```

This lists all the models available in the *nvidia/DeepLearningExamples:torchhub* repo, including WaveGlow, Tacotron 2, SSD, and others. Try using `hub.list()` on other repositories that support PyTorch Hub to see what other preexisting models you can find.

Loading preexisting and pretrained models from Python libraries like Torchvision and from repositories through PyTorch Hub allows you to build off previous research for your own work. Later in this chapter, I will show you how to deploy your models to packages and repositories so that others can access or build off your own research and development.

The PyTorch NN module (torch.nn)

One of the most powerful features of PyTorch is its Python module `torch.nn`, which makes it easy to design and experiment with new models. The following code illustrates how you can create a simple model with `torch.nn`. In this example, we will create a fully connected model called SimpleNet. It consists of an input layer, a hidden layer, and an output layer that takes in 2,048 input values and returns 2 output values for classification:

```
import torch.nn as nn
import torch.nn.functional as F

class SimpleNet(nn.Module):

    def __init__(self):  ❶
        super(SimpleNet, self).__init__()  ❷
        self.fc1 = nn.Linear(2048, 256)
        self.fc2 = nn.Linear(256, 64)
        self.fc3 = nn.Linear(64,2)

    def forward(self, x):  ❸
        x = x.view(-1, 2048)
        x = F.relu(self.fc1(x))
        x = F.relu(self.fc2(x))
        x = F.softmax(self.fc3(x),dim=1)
        return x
```

❶ Typically creates layers as class attributes

❷ Calls the base class's __init__() function to initialize parameters

❸ Required to define how the model processes data

Creating a model in PyTorch is said to be very "Pythonic," meaning it creates objects in the preferred Python fashion. We first create a new subclass called SimpleNet that inherits from the nn.Module class, and then we define the __init__() and for ward() methods. The __init__() function initializes the model parameters and the forward() function defines how data is passed through our model.

In __init__(), we call the super() function to execute the parent nn.Module class's __init__() method to initialize the class parameters. Then we define some layers using the nn.Linear module.

The forward() function defines how data is passed through the network. In the forward() function, we first use view() to reshape the input into a 2,048-element vector, then we process the input through each layer and apply relu() activation functions. Finally, we apply the softmax() function and return the output.

So far, we've defined what layers or modules are contained in our SimpleNet model, how they are connected, and how the parameters are initialized (through super().init()).

The following code shows how to create the model by instantiating the model object, called simplenet:

```
simplenet = SimpleNet()  ❶

print(simplenet)
# out:
# SimpleNet(
#   (fc1): Linear(in_features=2048,
#                 out_features=256, bias=True)
#   (fc2): Linear(in_features=256,
#                 out_features=64, bias=True)
#   (fc3): Linear(in_features=64,
#                 out_features=2, bias=True)
# )

input = torch.rand(2048)
output = simplenet(input)  ❷
```

❶ Instantiate or create the model.

❷ Run data through the model (forward pass).

If we print the model, we can see how it's structured. Executing our model is as simple as calling the model object as a function.

We pass in the inputs, and the model runs the forward pass and returns the outputs.

This simple model demonstrates the following decisions you need to make during model design:

Module definition
> How will you define the layers of your NN? How will you combine these layers into building blocks? In the example, we chose three linear or fully connected layers.

Activation functions
> Which activation functions will you use at the end of each layer or module? In the example, we chose to use relu activation for the input and hidden layers and softmax for the output layer.

Module connections
> How will your modules be connected to each other? In the example, we chose to simply connect each linear layer in sequence.

Output selection
> What output values and formats will be returned? In this example, we return two values from the softmax() function.

The simplicity, flexibility, and Pythonic nature of this paradigm are what make PyTorch so popular for deep learning research. PyTorch's torch.nn Python module includes classes for creating the building blocks, layers, and activation functions required for NN model design. Let's walk through the different types of building blocks available in PyTorch.

Table 3-2 provides a list of *NN containers*. You can use the container classes to create higher-level sets of building blocks. For example, you can use Sequential to create a sequence of layers in one block.

Table 3-2. PyTorch NN containers

Class	Description
Module	The base class for all NN modules
Sequential	A sequential container
ModuleList	A container that holds submodules in a list
ModuleDict	A container that holds submodules in a dictionary
ParameterList	A container that holds parameters in a list
ParameterDict	A container that holds parameters in a dictionary

---

NOTE

nn.Module is the base class for all NN building blocks. Your NN may consist of a single module or multiple modules containing other modules that may also contain modules, creating a hierarchy of building blocks.

Table 3-3 lists a few *linear layers* supported by torch.nn. Linear is commonly used for fully connected layers.

Table 3-3. PyTorch NN linear layers

Class	Description
nn.Identity	A placeholder identity operator that is argument-insensitive
nn.Linear	A layer that applies a linear transformation to the incoming data
nn.Bilinear	A layer that applies a bilinear transformation to the incoming data

Table 3-4 lists several *convolutional layers* supported by torch.nn. Convolutional layers are used often in deep learning to apply filters to data at various stages. As you can see in the table, PyTorch has built-in support for 1D, 2D, and 3D convolutions as well as transposed and folded variations.

Table 3-4. PyTorch NN convolutional layers

Class	Description
nn.Conv1d	Applies a 1D convolution over an input signal composed of several input planes
nn.Conv2d	Applies a 2D convolution over an input signal composed of several input planes
nn.Conv3d	Applies a 3D convolution over an input signal composed of several input planes
nn.ConvTranspose1d	Applies a 1D transposed convolution operator over an input image composed of several input planes
nn.ConvTranspose2d	Applies a 2D transposed convolution operator over an input image composed of several input planes
nn.ConvTranspose3d	Applies a 3D transposed convolution operator over an input image composed of several input planes
nn.Unfold	Extracts sliding local blocks from a batched-input tensor
nn.Fold	Combines an array of sliding local blocks into a large containing tensor

Table 3-5 shows the *pooling layers* available in torch.nn. Pooling is often used to downsample or reduce the complexity of output layers. PyTorch supports 1D, 2D, and 3D pooling and max or average pooling methods, including their adaptive variations.

Table 3-5. PyTorch NN pooling layers

Class	Description
nn.MaxPool1d	Applies a 1D max pooling over an input signal composed of several input planes
nn.MaxPool2d	Applies a 2D max pooling over an input signal composed of several input planes
nn.MaxPool3d	Applies a 3D max pooling over an input signal composed of several input planes

Class	Description
nn.MaxUnpool1d	Computes a partial inverse of MaxPool1d
nn.MaxUnpool2d	Computes a partial inverse of MaxPool2d
nn.MaxUnpool3d	Computes a partial inverse of MaxPool3d
nn.AvgPool1d	Applies a 1D average pooling over an input signal composed of several input planes
nn.AvgPool2d	Applies a 2D average pooling over an input signal composed of several input planes
nn.AvgPool3d	Applies a 3D average pooling over an input signal composed of several input planes
nn.FractionalMaxPool2d	Applies a 2D fractional max pooling over an input signal composed of several input planes
nn.LPPool1d	Applies a 1D power-average pooling over an input signal composed of several input planes
nn.LPPool2d	Applies a 2D power-average pooling over an input signal composed of several input planes
nn.AdaptiveMaxPool1d	Applies a 1D adaptive max pooling over an input signal composed of several input planes
nn.AdaptiveMaxPool2d	Applies a 2D adaptive max pooling over an input signal composed of several input planes
nn.AdaptiveMaxPool3d	Applies a 3D adaptive max pooling over an input signal composed of several input planes
nn.AdaptiveAvgPool1d	Applies a 1D adaptive average pooling over an input signal composed of several input planes
nn.AdaptiveAvgPool2d	Applies a 2D adaptive average pooling over an input signal composed of several input planes
nn.AdaptiveAvgPool3d	Applies a 3D adaptive average pooling over an input signal composed of several input planes

Table 3-6 lists the available *padding layers*. Padding fills in missing data when the layer outputs increase in size. PyTorch supports 1D, 2D, and 3D padding, and can pad your data with reflections, replications, zeros, or constants.

Table 3-6. PyTorch NN padding layers

Class	Description
nn.ReflectionPad1d	Pads the input tensor using the reflection of the input boundary
nn.ReflectionPad2d	Pads the input tensor using the reflection of the input boundary for 2D inputs
nn.ReplicationPad1d	Pads the input tensor using the replication of the input boundary
nn.ReplicationPad2d	Pads the input tensor using the replication of the input boundary for 2D inputs
nn.ReplicationPad3d	Pads the input tensor using the replication of the input boundary for 3D inputs
nn.ZeroPad2d	Pads the input tensor boundaries with zeros
nn.ConstantPad1d	Pads the input tensor boundaries with a constant value
nn.ConstantPad2d	Pads the input tensor boundaries with a constant value for 2D inputs
nn.ConstantPad3d	Pads the input tensor boundaries with a constant value for 3D inputs

Table 3-7 lists the available layers for *dropout*. Dropout is often used to reduce complexity, speed up training, and introduce some regularization to prevent overfitting. PyTorch supports dropout for 1D, 2D, and 3D layers, and provides support for alpha dropout as well.

Table 3-7. PyTorch NN dropout layers

Class	Description
nn.Dropout	During training, randomly zeros out some of the elements of the input tensor with probability p using samples from a Bernoulli distribution
nn.Dropout2d	Randomly zeros out entire channels for 2D inputs
nn.Dropout3d	Randomly zeros out entire channels for 3D inputs
nn.AlphaDropout	Applies alpha dropout over the input

Table 3-8 provides a list of classes that support *normalization*. Normalization is performed between some layers to prevent vanishing or exploding gradients by keeping intermediate layer inputs within a certain range. It can also help speed up the training process. PyTorch supports normalization for 1D, 2D, and 3D inputs and provides normalization methods such as batch, instance, group, and sync normalization.

Table 3-8. PyTorch NN normalization layers

Class	Description
nn.BatchNorm1d	Applies batch normalization over a 2D or 3D input (a mini-batch of 1D inputs with an optional additional channel dimension), as described in the paper "Batch Normalization: Accelerating Deep Network Training by Reducing Internal Covariate Shift"
nn.BatchNorm2d	Applies batch normalization over a 4D input (a mini-batch of 2D inputs with an additional channel dimension), as described in the paper "Batch Normalization"
nn.BatchNorm3d	Applies batch normalization over a 5D input (a mini-batch of 3D inputs with an additional channel dimension), as described in the paper "Batch Normalization"

Class	Description
nn.GroupNorm	Applies group normalization over a mini-batch of inputs as described in the paper "Group Normalization"
nn.SyncBatchNorm	Applies batch normalization over an n-dimensional input (a mini-batch of $[n-2]$D inputs with an additional channel dimension), as described in the paper "Batch Normalization"
nn.InstanceNorm1d	Applies instance normalization over a 3D input (a mini-batch of 1D inputs with an optional additional channel dimension), as described in the paper "Instance Normalization: The Missing Ingredient for Fast Stylization"
nn.InstanceNorm2d	Applies instance normalization over a 4D input (a mini-batch of 2D inputs with an additional channel dimension), as described in the paper "Instance Normalization"
nn.InstanceNorm3d	Applies instance normalization over a 5D input (a mini-batch of 3D inputs with an additional channel dimension), as described in the paper "Instance Normalization"
nn.LayerNorm	Applies layer normalization over a mini-batch of inputs, as described in the paper "Layer Normalization"
nn.LocalResponseNorm	Applies local response normalization over an input signal composed of several input planes, in which channels occupy the second dimension

Table 3-9 shows the *recurrent layers* used for recurrent neural networks (RNNs). RNNs are often used to process time series or sequence-based data. PyTorch has built-in support for RNN, long short-term memory (LSTM), and gated recurrent unit (GRU) layers as well as classes for RNN, LSTM, and GRU individual cells.

Table 3-9. PyTorch NN recurrent layers

Class	Description
nn.RNNBase	The RNN base class
nn.RNN	A layer that applies a multilayer Elman RNN with \Tanh or ReLU nonlinearity to an input sequence
nn.LSTM	A layer that applies a multilayer LSTM RNN to an input sequence
nn.GRU	A layer that applies a multilayer GRU RNN to an input sequence
nn.RNNCell	An Elman RNN cell with tanh or ReLU nonlinearity
nn.LSTMCell	An LSTM cell
nn.GRUCell	A GRU cell

Table 3-10 lists the *transformer layers* used for transformer networks. Transformer networks are often considered the state of the art for processing sequence data. PyTorch supports the complete Transformer model class in addition to providing the Encoder and Decoder submodules in stack and layer formats.

Table 3-10. PyTorch NN transformer layers

Class	Description
nn.Transformer	A transformer model
nn.TransformerEncoder	A stack of *N* encoder layers
nn.TransformerDecoder	A stack of *N* decoder layers
nn.TransformerEncoderLayer	A layer made up of a self-attention (attn) and feed-forward network
nn.TransformerDecoderLayer	A layer made up of a self-attn, multihead-attn, and feed-forward network

Table 3-11 contains a list of *sparse layers*. PyTorch provides built-in support for text data embeddings as well as sparse layers for cosine similarity and pairwise distance, often used in recommendation engine algorithms.

Table 3-11. PyTorch NN sparse layers and distance functions

Class	Description
nn.Embedding	Stores the embeddings of a fixed dictionary and size
nn.EmbeddingBag	Computes sums or means of "bags" of embeddings without instantiating the intermediate embeddings
nn.CosineSimilarity	Returns the cosine similarity between x_1 and x_2 computed along a dimension
nn.PairwiseDistance	Computes the batchwise pairwise distance between the vectors v_1 and v_2 using the p-norm

Table 3-12 contains a list of *vision layers* to support computer vision. They include layers to shuffle pixels and perform several upsampling algorithms.

Table 3-12. PyTorch NN vision layers

Class	Description
nn.PixelShuffle	Rearranges elements in a tensor of shape ($*$, $C \times r^2, H, W$) to a tensor of shape ($*$, C, $H \times r, W \times r$)
nn.Upsample	Upsamples the given multichannel 1D (temporal), 2D (spatial), or 3D (volumetric) data
nn.UpsamplingNearest2d	Applies a 2D nearest neighbor upsampling to an input signal composed of several input channels
nn.UpsamplingBilinear2d	Applies a 2D bilinear upsampling to an input signal composed of several input channels

Table 3-13 provides a list of all the *activations* available in torch.nn. Activation functions are often applied to layer outputs to introduce nonlinearities into a model. PyTorch supports traditional activations such as sigmoid, tanh, softmax, and ReLU as well as more recent functions such as leaky ReLU. More functions are being added as researchers design and apply new activations in their publications.

Table 3-13. PyTorch NN nonlinear activations

Class	Description
nn.ELU	Applies the exponential linear unit function element-wise
nn.Hardshrink	Applies the hard shrinkage function element-wise
nn.Hardsigmoid	Applies the hard sigmoid function element-wise
nn.Hardtanh	Applies the hardtanh function element-wise
nn.Hardswish	Applies the hardswish function element-wise
nn.LeakyReLU	Applies the leaky rectified linear unit function element-wise
nn.LogSigmoid	Applies the logarithmic sigmoid function element-wise
nn.MultiheadAttention	Allows the model to jointly attend to information from different representation subspaces
nn.PReLU	Applies the parametric rectified linear unit function element-wise
nn.ReLU	Applies the rectified linear unit function element-wise
nn.ReLU6	Applies the rectified linear unit function with a maximum
nn.RReLU	Applies the randomized leaky rectified liner unit function element-wise
nn.SELU	Applies the scaled exponential linear unit function element-wise

Class	Description
nn.CELU	Applies the continuously differentiable exponential linear unit function element-wise
nn.GELU	Applies the Gaussian error linear unit function
nn.Sigmoid	Applies the sigmoid function element-wise
nn.Softplus	Applies the softplus function element-wise
nn.Softshrink	Applies the soft shrinkage function element-wise
nn.Softsign	Applies the softsign function element-wise
nn.Tanh	Applies the hyperbolic tangent function element-wise
nn.Tanhshrink	Applies the hyperbolic tangent function with shrinkage element-wise
nn.Threshold	Establishes the threshold of each element of the input tensor
nn.Softmin	Applies the softmin function to an n-dimensional input tensor to rescale them so the elements of the n-dimensional output tensor lie in the range [0, 1] and sum to 1
nn.Softmax	Applies the softmax function to an n-dimensional input tensor to rescale them so the elements of the n-dimensional output tensor lie in the range [0,1] and sum to 1
nn.Softmax2d	Applies the softmax function to features in each spatial location
nn.LogSoftmax	Applies the $\log(\text{softmax}(x))$ function to an n-dimensional input tensor

Class	Description
`nn.AdaptiveLogSoftmax` `WithLoss`	Gives an efficient softmax approximation, as described in "Efficient Softmax Approximation for GPUs" by Edouard Grave et al.

As you can see, the PyTorch `torch.nn` module supports a robust set of NN layers and activation functions. You can use its classes to create everything from simple sequential models to complex multiple hierarchical networks, generative adversarial networks (GANs), transformer networks, RNNs, and more.

Now that you know how to design your model, let's explore how you can train and test your own NN model designs with PyTorch.

Training

During model design, you defined your NN modules, their parameters, and how they are connected to each other. In PyTorch, your model design is implemented as a model object derived from the `torch.nn.Module` class. You can call the object to pass data into the model and generate outputs based on the model architecture and the current values of its parameters.

The next step in model development is to train your model with your training data. Training a model involves nothing more than estimating the model's parameters, passing in data, and adjusting the parameters to achieve a more accurate representation of how the data is generally modeled.

In other words, you set the parameters to some values, pass through data, and then compare the model's outputs with true outputs to measure the error. The goal is to change the parameters and repeat the process until the error is minimized and the model's outputs are the same as the true outputs.

Fundamental training loop

One of the key advantages of PyTorch over other machine learning frameworks is its flexibility, especially when creating customized training loops. In this chapter, we'll explore a fundamental training loop commonly used for supervised learning.

In this example, we will train the LeNet5 model with the CIFAR-10 dataset that we used earlier in this chapter. The LeNet5 model is a simple convolutional NN developed by Yann LeCun and his team at Bell Labs in the 1990s to classify handwritten digits. (Unbeknownst to me at the time, I actually worked for Bell Labs in the same building in Holmdel, NJ, while this work was being performed.)

A modernized version of the LeNet5 model can be created using the following code:

```python
from torch import nn
import torch.nn.functional as F

class LeNet5(nn.Module):  ❶
    def __init__(self):
        super(LeNet5, self).__init__()
        self.conv1 = nn.Conv2d(3, 6, 5)
        self.conv2 = nn.Conv2d(6, 16, 5)
        self.fc1 = nn.Linear(16 * 5 * 5, 120)
        self.fc2 = nn.Linear(120, 84)
        self.fc3 = nn.Linear(84, 10)

    def forward(self, x):
        x = F.max_pool2d(F.relu(self.conv1(x)),
                         (2, 2))
        x = F.max_pool2d(F.relu(self.conv2(x)), 2)
        x = x.view(-1,
                   int(x.nelement() / x.shape[0]))
        x = F.relu(self.fc1(x))
        x = F.relu(self.fc2(x))
        x = self.fc3(x)
        return x

device = ('cuda' if torch.cuda.is_available()
    else 'cpu')  ❷
model = LeNet5().to(device=device)  ❸
```

❶ Define the model class.

❷ Use a GPU if it's available.

❸ Create the model and move it to a GPU (if available).

As shown in the preceding code, our LeNet5 model uses two convolutional layers and three fully connected or linear layers. It has been modernized with max pooling and ReLU activations. We'll also utilize a GPU for training in this example, if we can, to speed up training. Here, we create the model object, called model.

Next, we need to define the loss function (which is also called the *criterion*) and the optimizer algorithm. The loss function determines how we measure the performance of our model and computes the loss or error between predictions and truth. We'll attempt to minimize the loss by adjusting the model parameters during training. The optimizer defines how we update our model's parameters during training.

To define the loss function and the optimizer, we use the torch.optim and torch.nn packages as shown in the following code:

```
from torch import optim
from torch import nn

criterion = nn.CrossEntropyLoss()
optimizer = optim.SGD(model.parameters(),   ❶
                      lr=0.001,
                      momentum=0.9)
```

❶ Be sure to pass in the model.parameters() for your model.

For this example, we use the CrossEntropyLoss() function and the stochastic gradient descent (SGD) optimizer. Cross entropy loss is frequently used for classification problems. The SGD algorithm is also commonly used as an optimizer function. Choosing a loss function and an optimizer is beyond the scope of this book; however, we'll examine many built-in PyTorch loss functions and optimizers later in this chapter.

WARNING

PyTorch optimizers require that you pass in the model parameters using the `parameters()` method (i.e., `model.parameters()`). It's a common mistake to forget the ().

The following PyTorch code demonstrates the fundamental training loop:

```
N_EPOCHS = 10
for epoch in range(N_EPOCHS):  ❶

    epoch_loss = 0.0
    for inputs, labels in trainloader:
        inputs = inputs.to(device)  ❷
        labels = labels.to(device)

        optimizer.zero_grad()  ❸

        outputs = model(inputs)  ❹
        loss = criterion(outputs, labels)  ❺
        loss.backward()  ❻
        optimizer.step()  ❼

        epoch_loss += loss.item()  ❽
    print("Epoch: {} Loss: {}".format(epoch,
            epoch_loss/len(trainloader)))

# out: (results will vary and make take minutes)
# Epoch: 0 Loss: 1.8982970092773437
# Epoch: 1 Loss: 1.6062103009033204
# Epoch: 2 Loss: 1.484384165763855
# Epoch: 3 Loss: 1.3944422281837463
# Epoch: 4 Loss: 1.334191104450226
# Epoch: 5 Loss: 1.2834235876464843
# Epoch: 6 Loss: 1.2407222446250916
# Epoch: 7 Loss: 1.2081411465930938
```

```
# Epoch: 8 Loss: 1.1832368299865723
# Epoch: 9 Loss: 1.1534993273162841
```

❶ Outer training loop; loop over 10 epochs.

❷ Move inputs and labels to GPU if available.

❸ Zero out gradients before each backpropagation pass, or they'll accumulate.

❹ Perform forward pass.

❺ Compute loss.

❻ Perform backpropagation; compute gradients.

❼ Adjust parameters based on gradients.

❽ Accumulate batch loss so we can average over the epoch.

The training loop consists of two loops. In the outer loop, we will process the entire set of training data during every iteration or epoch. However, instead of waiting to process the entire dataset before updating the model's parameters, we process smaller batches of data, one batch at a time. The inner loop loops over each batch.

WARNING

By default, PyTorch accumulates the gradients during each call to `loss.backward()` (i.e., the backward pass). This is convenient while training some types of NNs, such as RNNs; however, it is not desired for convolutional neural networks (CNNs). In most cases, you will need to call `optimizer.zero_grad()` to zero the gradients before doing backpropagation so the optimizer updates the model parameters correctly.

For each batch, we pass the batch (called `inputs`) into the model. It runs the forward pass and returns the computed outputs. Next, we compare the model outputs (called `outputs`) with the true values from the training dataset (called `labels`) using `criterion()` to compute the error or loss.

Next, we adjust the model parameters (i.e., the weights and biases of the NN) to reduce the loss. To do so, we first perform backpropagation with `loss.backward()` to compute the gradients and then run the optimizer with `optimizer.step()` to update the parameters based on the computed gradients.

This is the fundamental process used for training NN models. Implementations may vary, but you can use this example as a quick reference when creating your own training loops. When designing the training loop, you will need to decide how data will be processed or batched, what loss function to use, and what optimizer algorithm to run.

You can use one of PyTorch's built-in loss functions and optimizer algorithms, or you can create your own.

Loss functions

PyTorch includes many built-in loss functions in the `torch.nn` Python module. Table 3-14 provides a list of available loss functions.

Table 3-14. Loss functions

Loss function	Description
`nn.L1Loss()`	Creates a criterion that measures the mean absolute error (MAE) between each element in the input x and target y
`nn.MSELoss()`	Creates a criterion that measures the mean squared error (squared L2 norm) between each element in the input x and target y

Loss function	Description
nn.CrossEntropyLoss()	Combines nn.LogSoftmax() and nn.NLLLoss() in a single class
nn.CTCLoss()	Calculates the connectionist temporal classification loss
nn.NLLLoss()	Calculates the negative log likelihood loss
nn.PoissonNLLLoss()	Calculates the negative log likelihood loss with a Poisson distribution of the target
nn.KLDivLoss()	Measures the Kullback–Leibler divergence loss
nn.BCELoss()	Creates a criterion that measures the binary cross entropy between the target and the output
nn.BCEWithLogitsLoss()	Combines a sigmoid layer and the nn.BCELoss() in a single class
nn.MarginRankingLoss()	Creates a criterion that measures the loss when given inputs x^1, x^2, two 1D mini-batch tensors, and a label 1D mini-batch tensor y (containing 1 or −1)
nn.HingeEmbeddingLoss()	Measures the loss when given an input tensor x and a label tensor y (containing 1 or −1)
nn.MultiLabelMarginLoss()	Creates a criterion that optimizes a multiclass classification hinge loss (i.e., a margin-based loss) between input x (a 2D mini-batch tensor) and output y (a 2D tensor of target class indices)

Loss function	Description
nn.SmoothL1Loss()	Creates a criterion that uses a squared term if the absolute element-wise error falls below 1 or an L1 term otherwise
nn.SoftMarginLoss()	Creates a criterion that optimizes a two-class classification logistic loss between input tensor x and target tensor y (containing 1 or -1)
nn.MultiLabelSoftMarginLoss()	Creates a criterion that optimizes a multilabel one-versus-all loss based on the maximum entropy
nn.CosineEmbeddingLoss()	Creates a criterion that measures the loss given input tensors x^1, x^2 and a tensor labeled y with values 1 or -1
nn.MultiMarginLoss()	Creates a criterion that optimizes a multiclass classification hinge loss
nn.TripletMarginLoss()	Creates a criterion that measures the triplet loss when given input tensors x^1, x^2, x^3 and a margin with a value greater than 0

WARNING

The CrossEntropyLoss() function includes the softmax calculation, which is usually performed in the last step of an NN classifier model. When using CrossEntropyLoss(), do not include Softmax() in the output layer of your model definition.

Optimizer algorithms

PyTorch also includes many built-in optimizer algorithms in the `torch.optim` Python submodule. Table 3-15 lists the available optimizer algorithms and their descriptions.

Table 3-15. Optimizer algorithms

Algorithm	Description
Adadelta()	An adaptive learning rate method
Adagrad()	An adaptive gradient algorithm
Adam()	A method for stochastic optimization
AdamW()	An Adam variant proposed in "Decoupled Weight Decay Regularization" (*https://arxiv.org/abs/1711.05101*)
SparseAdam()	A version of Adam suitable for sparse tensors
Adamax()	A variant of Adam based on the infinity norm
ASGD()	Averaged stochastic gradient descent
LBFGS()	A limited-memory implementation of the BFGS algorithm, heavily inspired by minFunc (*https://www.cs.ubc.ca/~schmidtm/Software/minFunc.html*)
RMSprop()	Root mean square propagation
Rprop()	Resilient backpropagation
SGD()	Stochastic gradient descent

The `torch.optim` Python submodule supports most commonly used algorithms. The interface is general enough so new ones can also be easily integrated in the future. Visit the `torch.optim` documentation (*https://pytorch.org/docs/stable/optim.html*) for more details on how to configure the algorithms and adjust their learning rates.

Validation

Now that we have trained our model and attempted to minimize the loss, how can we evaluate its performance? How do we know that our model will generalize and work with data it has never seen before?

Model development often includes validation and testing loops to ensure that overfitting does not occur and that the model will perform well against unseen data. Let's address validation first. Here, I'll provide you with a quick reference for how you can add validation to your training loops with PyTorch.

Typically, we will reserve a portion of the training data for validation. The validation data will not be used to train the NN; instead, we'll use it to test the performance of the model at the end of each epoch.

Validation is good practice when training your models. It's commonly performed when adjusting hyperparameters. For example, maybe we want to slow down the learning rate after five epochs.

Before we perform validation, we need to split our training dataset into a training dataset and a validation dataset, as shown in the following code:

```
from torch.utils.data import random_split

train_set, val_set = random_split(
                        train_data,
                        [40000, 10000])

trainloader = torch.utils.data.DataLoader(
                        train_set,
                        batch_size=16,
                        shuffle=True)

valloader = torch.utils.data.DataLoader(
                        val_set,
                        batch_size=16,
                        shuffle=True)

print(len(trainloader))
# out: 2500
```

```
print(len(valloader))
# out: 625
```

We use the `random_split()` function from `torch.utils.data` to reserve 10,000 of our 50,000 training images for validation. Once we create our `train_set` and `val_set`, we create our dataloaders for each one.

We then define our model, loss function (or criterion), and optimizer, as shown here:

```
from torch import optim
from torch import nn

model = LeNet5().to(device)
criterion = nn.CrossEntropyLoss()
optimizer = optim.SGD(model.parameters(),
                      lr=0.001,
                      momentum=0.9)
```

The following code shows the previous fundamental training example with validation added:

```
N_EPOCHS = 10
for epoch in range(N_EPOCHS):

    # Training
    train_loss = 0.0
    model.train() ❶
    for inputs, labels in trainloader:
        inputs = inputs.to(device)
        labels = labels.to(device)

        optimizer.zero_grad()

        outputs = model(inputs)
        loss = criterion(outputs, labels)
        loss.backward()
        optimizer.step()

        train_loss += loss.item()

    # Validation
    val_loss = 0.0
    model.eval() ❷
    for inputs, labels in valloader:
        inputs = inputs.to(device)
        labels = labels.to(device)
```

```
        outputs = model(inputs)
        loss = criterion(outputs, labels)

        val_loss += loss.item()

    print(
        "Epoch: {} Train Loss: {} Val Loss: {}".format(
                    epoch,
                    train_loss/len(trainloader),
                    val_loss/len(valloader)))
```

❶ Configure the model for training.

❷ Configure the model for testing.

Validation occurs at every epoch after the training data has been processed. During validation, the model is passed data that was not used in training and that has not yet been seen by the model. We only perform the forward pass during validation.

NOTE

Running the .train() or .eval() method on your model object puts the model in training or testing mode, respectively. Calling these methods is only necessary if your model operates differently for training and evaluation. For example, dropout and batch normalization are used in training but not in validation or testing. It's good practice to call .train() and .eval() in your loops.

If the loss decreases for validation data, then the model is doing well. However, if the training loss decreases but the validation loss does not, then there's a good chance the model is overfitting. Look at your results from the previous training loop. You should have similar results to the following:

```
# out: (results may vary and take a few minutes)
# Epoch: 0 Train Loss: 1.987607608 Val Loss: 1.740786979
# Epoch: 1 Train Loss: 1.649753892 Val Loss: 1.587019552
```

```
# Epoch: 2 Train Loss: 1.511723689 Val Loss: 1.435539366
# Epoch: 3 Train Loss: 1.408525426 Val Loss: 1.361453659
# Epoch: 4 Train Loss: 1.339505518 Val Loss: 1.293459154
# Epoch: 5 Train Loss: 1.290560259 Val Loss: 1.245048282
# Epoch: 6 Train Loss: 1.259268565 Val Loss: 1.285989610
# Epoch: 7 Train Loss: 1.235161985 Val Loss: 1.253840940
# Epoch: 8 Train Loss: 1.207051850 Val Loss: 1.215700019
# Epoch: 9 Train Loss: 1.189215132 Val Loss: 1.183332257
```

As you can see, our model is training well and does not seem to be overfitting, since both the training loss and the validation loss are decreasing. If we train the model for more epochs, we may get even better results.

We're not quite finished, though. Our model may still be overfitting. We might have just gotten lucky with our choice of hyperparameters, leading to good validation results. As a further test against overfitting, we will run some test data through our model.

The model has never seen the test data during training, nor has the test data had any influence on the hyperparameters. Let's see how we perform against the test dataset.

Testing

CIFAR-10 provides its own test dataset, and we created test_data and a testloader earlier in the chapter. Let's run the test data through our test loop, as shown in the following code:

```
num_correct = 0.0
for x_test_batch, y_test_batch in testloader:
  model.eval() ❶
  y_test_batch = y_test_batch.to(device)
  x_test_batch = x_test_batch.to(device)
  y_pred_batch = model(x_test_batch) ❷
  _, predicted = torch.max(y_pred_batch, 1) ❸
  num_correct += (predicted ==
    y_test_batch).float().sum() ❹

accuracy = num_correct/(len(testloader) \
  *testloader.batch_size) ❺

print(len(testloader), testloader.batch_size)
# out: 625 16
```

```
print("Test Accuracy: {}".format(accuracy))
# out: Test Accuracy: 0.6322000026702881
```

❶ Set the model to evaluation mode for testing.

❷ Predict the outcomes for each batch.

❸ Select the class index with the highest probability.

❹ Compare the prediction to the true label and count the number of correct predictions.

❺ Compute the percentage of correct predictions (accuracy).

Our initial test results after 10 epochs of training show a 63% accuracy rate against the test data. That's not a bad start; see if you can improve the accuracy by training over more epochs.

You now know how to create training, validation, and test loops using PyTorch. Feel free to use this code as a reference when creating your own loops.

Now that you have a fully trained model, let's explore what you can do with it in the model deployment stage.

Model Deployment

Depending upon your goals, there are many options for saving or deploying your trained models. If you are conducting deep learning research, you may want to save your models in such a way that you can repeat your experiments or access them later for presentations and publishing papers. You may also wish to publish your models as part of a Python package like Torchvision or release them to a repository like PyTorch Hub so that other researchers can access your work.

On the development side, you may want to deploy your trained NN model to a production environment or integrate your model with a product or service. This could be a prototype system, edge device, or mobile device. You may also want to deploy it to a local production server or a cloud server that provides an API endpoint that a system can use. Whatever your goal, PyTorch provides capabilities to help you deploy your models as you wish.

Saving Models

One of the simplest things you can do is save your trained model for future use. When you want to run your model against new inputs, you can simply load it and call the model with the new values.

The following code illustrates the recommended way to save and load a trained model. It uses the `state_dict()` method, which creates a dictionary object that maps each layer to its parameter tensor. In other words, we only need to save the model's learned parameters. We already have the model's design defined in our model class, so we don't need to save the architecture. When we load the model, we use the constructor to create a "blank model," and then we use `load_state_dict()` to set the parameters for each layer:

```
torch.save(model.state_dict(), "./lenet5_model.pt")

model = LeNet5().to(device)
model.load_state_dict(torch.load("./lenet5_model.pt"))
```

Note that `load_state_dict()` requires a dictionary object, not a path to a saved `state_dict` object. You must use `torch.load()` to deserialize the saved *state_dict* file before passing it to `load_state_dict()`.

NOTE

A common PyTorch convention is to save models using either a *.pt* or *.pth* file extension.

You can save and load the entire model using `torch.save(PATH)` and `model = torch.load(PATH)` too. Although this is more intuitive, it is not recommended because the serialization process is bound to the exact file path and directory structure used to define the model class. Your code can break if you refactor your class code and try to load the model in other projects. Saving and loading the `state_dict` object instead will give you more flexibility to restore the model later.

Deploying to PyTorch Hub

PyTorch Hub is a pretrained model repository designed to facilitate research reproducibility. Earlier in this chapter, I showed you how to load a preexisting or pretrained model from PyTorch Hub. Now, I'll show you how to publish your pretrained models, including model definitions and pretrained weights, to a GitHub repository by adding a simple *hubconf.py* file. The *hubconf.py* file defines the code dependencies and provides one or more endpoints to the PyTorch API.

In most cases just importing the right function will be sufficient, but you can define the entry point explicitly. The following code shows how you would load a model from PyTorch Hub using the VGG16 endpoint:

```
import torch
vgg16 = torch.hub.load('pytorch/vision',
  'vgg16', pretrained=True)
```

Now, if you had created VGG16 and wanted to deploy it to PyTorch Hub, all you would need to do is include the following *hubconf.py* file in the root of your repository. The *hubconf.py* configuration file sets `torch` as a dependency. Any function defined in this file will act as an endpoint, so simply importing the VGG16 function does the job:

```
dependencies = ['torch']
from torchvision.models.vgg import vgg16
```

If you want to explicitly define the endpoint, you can write a function like the one in the following code:

```
dependencies = ['torch']
from torchvision.models.vgg import vgg16 as _vgg16

# vgg16 is the name of the entrypoint
def vgg16(pretrained=False, **kwargs):
    """ # This docstring shows up in hub.help():
    VGG16 model
    pretrained (bool): kwargs,
      load pretrained weights into the model
    """
    # Call the model; load pretrained weights
    model = _vgg16(pretrained=pretrained, **kwargs)
    return model
```

And that's it! Researchers around the world will rejoice as they easily load your pretrained models from PyTorch Hub.

Deploying to Production

Saving models to files and repositories may be fine when you're conducting research; however, to solve most problems, we must integrate our models into products and services. This is often called "deploying to production." There are many ways to do this, and PyTorch has built-in capabilities to support them. Deploying to production is a comprehensive topic that will be discussed in depth in Chapter 7.

This chapter covered a lot of ground, exploring the deep learning development process and providing a quick reference to the PyTorch capabilities for implementing each step. The next chapter presents additional reference designs that you can use for projects involving transfer learning, sentiment analysis, and generative learning .

## CHAPTER 4

Neural Network Development Reference Designs

In the previous chapter we covered NN development process at a high level, and you learned how to implement each stage in PyTorch. The examples in that chapter focused on solving an image classification problem with the CIFAR-10 dataset and a simple fully connected network. CIFAR-10 image classification is a good academic example to illustrate the NN development process, but there's a lot more to developing deep learning models with PyTorch.

This chapter presents some additional reference designs for NN development with PyTorch. Reference designs are code examples that you can use as a reference to solve similar types of problems.

Indeed, the set of reference designs in this chapter merely scratches the surface when it comes to the possibilities of deep learning; however, I'll attempt to provide you with enough variety to assist you in the development of your own solutions. We will use three examples to process a variety of data, design different model architectures, and explore other approaches to the learning process.

The first example uses PyTorch to perform transfer learning to classify images of bees and ants with a small dataset and a pre-trained network. The second example uses PyTorch to perform sentiment analysis using text data to train an NLP model that predicts the positive or negative sentiment of movie reviews. And the third example uses PyTorch to demonstrate generative learning by training a generative adversarial network (GAN) to generate images of articles of clothing.

In each example, I'll provide PyTorch code so that you can use this chapter as a quick reference when writing code for your own designs. Let's begin by seeing how PyTorch can solve a computer vision problem using transfer learning.

Image Classification with Transfer Learning

The subject of image classification has been studied in depth, and many famous models, like the AlexNet and VGG models we saw earlier, are readily available through PyTorch. However, these models have been trained with the ImageNet dataset. Although ImageNet contains 1,000 different image classes, it may not contain the classes that you need to solve your image classification problem.

In this case, you can apply *transfer learning*, a process in which we fine-tune pretrained models with a much smaller dataset of new images. For our next example, we will train a model to classify images of bees and ants—classes not contained in ImageNet. Bees and ants look very similar and can be difficult to distinguish.

To train our new classifier, we will fine-tune another famous model, called ResNet18, by loading the pretrained model and training it with 120 new training images of bees and ants—a much smaller set compared to the millions of images in ImageNet.

Data Processing

Let's begin by loading our data, defining our transforms, and configuring our dataloaders for batch sampling. As we did earlier, we'll leverage functions from the Torchvision library for creating the datasets, loading the data, and applying the data transforms.

First let's import the required libraries for this example:

```
import torch
import torch.nn as nn
import torch.optim as optim
import numpy as np
import torchvision
from torchvision import datasets, models
from torchvision import transforms
```

Then we'll download the data that we'll use for training and validation:

```
from io import BytesIO
from urllib.request import urlopen
from zipfile import ZipFile

zipurl = 'https://pytorch.tips/bee-zip'
with urlopen(zipurl) as zipresp:
  with ZipFile(BytesIO(zipresp.read())) as zfile:
      zfile.extractall('./data')
```

Here, we use the io, urlib, and zipfile libraries to download and unzip a file to our local filesystem. After running the previous code, you should have your training and validation images in your local *data/* folder. They are located in *data/hymenoptera_data/train* and *data/hymenoptera_data/val*, respectively.

Next let's define our transforms, load the data, and configure our batch samplers.

First we'll define our transforms:

```
train_transforms = transforms.Compose([
    transforms.RandomResizedCrop(224),
    transforms.RandomHorizontalFlip(),
    transforms.ToTensor(),
    transforms.Normalize(
        [0.485, 0.456,0.406],
        [0.229, 0.224, 0.225])])

val_transforms = transforms.Compose([
    transforms.Resize(256),
    transforms.CenterCrop(224),
    transforms.ToTensor(),
    transforms.Normalize(
        [0.485, 0.456, 0.406],
        [0.229, 0.224, 0.225])])
```

Notice that we randomly resize, crop, and flip images for training but not for validation. The "magic" numbers used in the
Normalize transforms are precomputed values for the means
and standard deviations.

Now let's define the datasets:

```
train_dataset = datasets.ImageFolder(
            root='data/hymenoptera_data/train',
            transform=train_transforms)

val_dataset = datasets.ImageFolder(
            root='data/hymenoptera_data/val',
            transform=val_transforms)
```

In the previous code we used the ImageFolder dataset to pull
images from our data folders and set the transforms to the ones
we defined earlier. Next, we define our dataloaders for batch
iteration:

```
train_loader = torch.utils.data.DataLoader(
            train_dataset,
            batch_size=4,
            shuffle=True,
            num_workers=4)

val_loader = torch.utils.data.DataLoader(
            val_dataset,
            batch_size=4,
```

```
                shuffle=True,
                num_workers=4)
```

We're using a batch size of 4, and we set `num_workers` to 4 to configure four CPU processes to handle the parallel processing.

Now that we have prepared our training and validation data, we can design our model.

Model Design

For this example we'll use a ResNet18 model that has been pretrained with ImageNet data. However, ResNet18 is designed to detect 1,000 classes, and in our case, we only need 2 classes—bees and ants. We can modify the final layer to detect 2 classes instead of 1,000 as shown in the following code:

```
model = models.resnet18(pretrained=True)

print(model.fc)
# out:
# Linear(in_features=512, out_features=1000, bias=True)

num_ftrs = model.fc.in_features
model.fc = nn.Linear(num_ftrs, 2)
print(model.fc)
# out:
# Linear(in_features=512, out_features=2, bias=True)
```

We first load a pretrained ResNet18 model using the function `torchvision.models.resnet18()`. Next, we read the number of features before the final layer with `model.fc.in_features`. Then we change the final layer by directly setting `model.fc` to a fully connected layer with two outputs.

We are going to use the pretrained model as a starting point and fine-tune its parameters with new data. Since we replaced the final linear layer, its parameters are now randomly initialized.

Now we have a ResNet18 model with all weights pretrained with ImageNet images except for the last layer. Next, we need to train our model with images of bees and ants.

Torchvision provides many famous pretrained models for computer vision and image processing, including the following:

- AlexNet
- VGG
- ResNet
- SqueezeNet
- DenseNet
- Inception v3
- GoogLeNet
- ShuffleNet v2
- MobileNet v2
- ResNeXt
- Wide ResNet
- MNASNet

For more information, explore the `torchvision.models` class or visit the Torchvision models documentation (*https://pytorch.tips/torchvision-models*).

Training and Validation

Before we fine-tune our model, let's configure our training with the following code:

```
from torch.optim.lr_scheduler import StepLR

device = torch.device("cuda:0" if
  torch.cuda.is_available() else "cpu") ❶

model = model.to(device)
criterion = nn.CrossEntropyLoss() ❷
optimizer = optim.SGD(model.parameters(),
```

```
                        lr=0.001,
                        momentum=0.9) ❸
  exp_lr_scheduler = StepLR(optimizer,
                            step_size=7,
                            gamma=0.1) ❹
```

❶ Move the model to a GPU if available.

❷ Define our loss function.

❸ Define our optimizer algorithm.

❹ Use a learning rate scheduler.

The code should look familiar, with the exception of the learning rate scheduler. Here we will use a scheduler from PyTorch to adjust the learning rate of our SGD optimizer after several epochs. Using a learning rate scheduler will help our NN adjust its weights more precisely as training goes on.

The following code illustrates the entire training loop, including validation:

```
num_epochs=25

for epoch in range(num_epochs):

  model.train() ❶
  running_loss = 0.0
  running_corrects = 0

  for inputs, labels in train_loader:
    inputs = inputs.to(device)
    labels = labels.to(device)

    optimizer.zero_grad()
    outputs = model(inputs)
    _, preds = torch.max(outputs,1)
    loss = criterion(outputs, labels)

    loss.backward()
    optimizer.step()

    running_loss += loss.item()/inputs.size(0)
    running_corrects += \
      torch.sum(preds == labels.data) \
```

```
            /inputs.size(0)

        exp_lr_scheduler.step() ❷
        train_epoch_loss = \
          running_loss / len(train_loader)
        train_epoch_acc = \
          running_corrects / len(train_loader)

        model.eval() ❸
        running_loss = 0.0
        running_corrects = 0

        for inputs, labels in val_loader:
            inputs = inputs.to(device)
            labels = labels.to(device)
            outputs = model(inputs)
            _, preds = torch.max(outputs,1)
            loss = criterion(outputs, labels)

            running_loss += loss.item()/inputs.size(0)
            running_corrects += \
              torch.sum(preds == labels.data) \
                /inputs.size(0)

        epoch_loss = running_loss / len(val_loader)
        epoch_acc = \
          running_corrects.double() / len(val_loader)
        print("Train: Loss: {:.4f} Acc: {:.4f}"
          " Val: Loss: {:.4f}"
          " Acc: {:.4f}".format(train_epoch_loss,
                                 train_epoch_acc,
                                 epoch_loss,
                                 epoch_acc))
```

❶ Training loop.

❷ Schedule the learning rate for next the epoch of training.

❸ Validation loop.

We should see the training and validation loss decrease while the accuracies improve. The results may bounce around a little.

Testing and Deployment

Let's test our model and deploy it by saving the model to a file. To test our model, we'll display a batch of images and show how our model classified them, as shown in the following code:

```
import matplotlib.pyplot as plt

def imshow(inp, title=None): ❶
    inp = inp.numpy().transpose((1, 2, 0)) ❷
    mean = np.array([0.485, 0.456, 0.406])
    std = np.array([0.229, 0.224, 0.225])
    inp = std * inp + mean ❸
    inp = np.clip(inp, 0, 1)
    plt.imshow(inp)
    if title is not None:
        plt.title(title)

inputs, classes = next(iter(val_loader)) ❹
out = torchvision.utils.make_grid(inputs)
class_names = val_dataset.classes

outputs = model(inputs.to(device)) ❺
_, preds = torch.max(outputs,1) ❻

imshow(out, title=[class_names[x] for x in preds]) ❼
```

❶ Define a new function to plot images from our tensor images.

❷ Switch from C × H × W to H × W × C image formats for plotting.

❸ Undo the normalization we do during transforms so we can properly view images.

❹ Grab a batch of images from our validation dataset.

❺ Perform classification using our fine-tuned ResNet18.

❻ Take the "winning" class.

❼ Display the input images and their predicted classes.

Since we have such a small dataset, we simply test the model by visualizing the output to make sure the images match the labels. Figure 4-1 shows an example test. Your results will vary since the `val_loader` will return a randomly sampled batch of images.

Figure 4-1. Results of image classification

When we are done, we save the model:

```
torch.save(model.state_dict(), "./resnet18.pt")
```

You can use this reference design for other cases of transfer learning, not only with image classification but with other types of data as well. As long as you can find a suitable pre-trained model, you will be able to modify the model and retrain only a portion of it with a small amount of data.

This example was based on the "*Transfer Learning for Computer Vision Tutorial*" (*https://pytorch.tips/transfer-learning-tutorial*) by Sasank Chilamkurthy. You can find more details in the tutorial.

Next, we'll venture into the field of NLP and explore a reference design that processes text data.

Sentiment Analysis with Torchtext

Another popular deep learning application is *sentiment analysis*, in which people classify a block of text data. In this example, we will train an NN to predict whether a movie review is either positive or negative using the well-known Internet Movie Database (IMDb) dataset. Sentiment analysis of IMDb data is a common beginner example for learning NLP.

Data Processing

The IMDb dataset consists of 25,000 movie reviews from IMDb that are labeled by sentiment (e.g., positive or negative). The PyTorch project includes a library called *Torchtext* that provides convenient capabilities for performing deep learning on text data. To begin our example reference design, we will use Torchtext to load and preprocess the IMDb dataset.

Before we load the dataset, we will define a function called `generate_bigrams()` that we'll use to preprocess our text review data. The model that we'll use for this example computes *n*-grams of an input sentence and appends them to the end. We'll use bi-grams, which are pairs of words or tokens that appear in a sentence.

The following code shows our preprocessing function, `generate_bigrams()`, and provides an example of how it works:

```
def generate_bigrams(x):
  n_grams = set(zip(*[x[i:] for i in range(2)]))
  for n_gram in n_grams:
    x.append(' '.join(n_gram))
  return x

generate_bigrams([
        'This', 'movie', 'is', 'awesome'])
# out:
# ['This', 'movie', 'is', 'awesome', 'This movie',
#  'movie is', 'is awesome']
```

Now that we have defined our preprocessing function, we can build our IMDb datasets as shown in the following code:

```
from torchtext.datasets import IMDB
from torch.utils.data.dataset import random_split

train_iter, test_iter = IMDB(
    split=('train', 'test')) ❶

train_dataset = list(train_iter) ❷
test_data = list(test_iter)

num_train = int(len(train_dataset) * 0.70)
train_data, valid_data = \
```

```
random_split(train_dataset,
    [num_train,
     len(train_dataset) - num_train]) ❸
```

❶ Load data from IMDb dataset.

❷ Redefine iterators as lists.

❸ Split training data into two sets, 70% for training and 30% for validation.

In the code, we load the training and test datasets using the IMDB class. We then use the random_split() function to break the training data into two smaller sets for training and validation.

WARNING

The Torchtext API changed significantly in PyTorch 1.8. Be sure you are using at least Torchtext 0.9 when running the code.

Let's take a quick look at the data:

```
print(len(train_data), len(valid_data),
  len(test_data))
# out:17500 7500 25000

data_index = 21
print(train_data[data_index][0])
# out: (your results may vary)
#   pos

print(train_data[data_index][1])
# out: (your results may vary)
# ['This', 'film', 'moved', 'me', 'beyond', ...
```

As you can see, our datasets have 17,500 reviews for training, 7,500 for validation, and 25,000 for testing. We also printed out the 21st review and its sentiment, as shown in the output. The splits are randomly sampled, so your results may be different.

Next we need to convert our text data into numerical data so that an NN can process it. We do this by creating preprocessing functions and a data pipeline. The data pipeline will use our generate_bigrams() function, a tokenizer, and a vocabulary, as shown in the following code:

```python
from torchtext.data.utils import get_tokenizer
from collections import Counter
from torchtext.vocab import Vocab

tokenizer = get_tokenizer('spacy')  ❶
counter = Counter()
for (label, line) in train_data:
    counter.update(generate_bigrams(
        tokenizer(line)))  ❷
vocab = Vocab(counter,
              max_size = 25000,
              vectors = "glove.6B.100d",
              unk_init = torch.Tensor.normal_,)  ❸
```

❶ Define our tokenizer (how to break up text).

❷ Make a list of all the tokens used in our training data and count how many times each occurs.

❸ Create a vocabulary (list of possible tokens) and define how tokens are converted to numbers.

In the code, we define the instructions for converting text to tensors. For the review text, we specify *spaCy* as the tokenizer. spaCy is a popular Python package for NLP and includes its own tokenizer. A tokenizer breaks text into components like words and punctuation marks.

We also create a vocabulary and an embedding. A vocabulary is just a set of words that we can use. If we find a word in the movie review that is not contained in the vocabulary, we set the word to a special word called "unknown." We limit our dictionary to 25,000 words, much smaller than the full set of words in the English language.

We also specify our vocabulary vectors, which causes us to download a pretrained embedding called GloVe (Global

Vectors for Word Representation) with 100 dimensions. It may take several minutes to download the GloVe data and create a vocabulary.

An embedding is a method to map a word or series of words to a numeric vector. Defining a vocabulary and an embedding is a complex topic and is beyond the scope of this book. For this example, we'll just build a vocabulary from our training data and download the popular pretrained GloVe embedding.

Now that we have defined our tokenizer and vocabulary, we can build our data pipelines for the review and label text data, as shown in the following code:

```
text_pipeline = lambda x: [vocab[token]
    for token in generate_bigrams(tokenizer(x))]

label_pipeline = lambda x: 1 if x=='pos' else 0

print(text_pipeline('the movie was horrible'))
# out:

print(label_pipeline('neg'))
# out:
```

We use `lambda` functions to pass text data through the pipeline so that PyTorch dataloaders can convert each text review to a 100-element vector.

Now that we have defined our datasets and preprocessing, we can create our dataloaders. Our dataloaders load batches of data from a sampling of the dataset and preprocess the data, as in the following code:

```
from torch.utils.data import DataLoader
from torch.nn.utils.rnn import pad_sequence

device = torch.device("cuda" if
    torch.cuda.is_available() else "cpu")

def collate_batch(batch):
    label_list, text_list = [], []
    for (_label, _text) in batch:
        label_list.append(label_pipeline(_label))
        processed_text = torch.tensor(
                         text_pipeline(_text))
```

```python
            text_list.append(processed_text)
    return (torch.tensor(label_list,
            dtype=torch.float64).to(device),
            pad_sequence(text_list,
                         padding_value=1.0).to(device))

batch_size = 64
def batch_sampler():
    indices = [(i, len(tokenizer(s[1])))
                for i, s in enumerate(train_dataset)]
    random.shuffle(indices)
    pooled_indices = []
    # create pool of indices with similar lengths
    for i in range(0, len(indices), batch_size * 100):
        pooled_indices.extend(sorted(
            indices[i:i + batch_size * 100], key=lambda x: x[1]))

    pooled_indices = [x[0] for x in pooled_indices]

    # yield indices for current batch
    for i in range(0, len(pooled_indices),
      batch_size):
        yield pooled_indices[i:i + batch_size]

BATCH_SIZE = 64

train_dataloader = DataLoader(train_data,
                    # batch_sampler=batch_sampler(),
                    collate_fn=collate_batch,
                    batch_size=BATCH_SIZE,
                    shuffle=True)
                    # collate_fn=collate_batch)
valid_dataloader = DataLoader(valid_data,
                    batch_size=BATCH_SIZE,
                    shuffle=True,
                    collate_fn=collate_batch)
test_dataloader = DataLoader(test_data,
                    batch_size=BATCH_SIZE,
                    shuffle=True,
                    collate_fn=collate_batch)
```

In the code, we set the batch size to 64 and use a GPU if available. We also define a collation function called col late_batch() and pass it into our dataloaders to execute our data pipelines.

Now that we have configured our pipelines and dataloaders, let's define our model.

Model Design

For this example we will use a model called FastText from the paper "Bag of Tricks for Efficient Text Classification" (*https://pytorch.tips/bag-of-tricks*) by Armand Joulin et al. While many sentiment analysis models use RNNs, this model uses a simpler approach instead.

The following code implements the FastText model:

```python
import torch.nn as nn
import torch.nn.functional as F

class FastText(nn.Module):
    def __init__(self,
                 vocab_size,
                 embedding_dim,
                 output_dim,
                 pad_idx):
        super().__init__()
        self.embedding = nn.Embedding(
            vocab_size,
            embedding_dim,
            padding_idx=pad_idx)
        self.fc = nn.Linear(embedding_dim,
                            output_dim)

    def forward(self, text):
        embedded = self.embedding(text)
        embedded = embedded.permute(1, 0, 2)
        pooled = F.avg_pool2d(
            embedded,
            (embedded.shape[1], 1)).squeeze(1)
        return self.fc(pooled)
```

As you can see, the model calculates the word embedding for each word using the nn.Embedded layer, and then it calculates the average of all the word embeddings with the avg_pool2d() function. Finally, it feeds the average through a linear layer. Refer to the paper for more details on this model.

Let's build our model with its appropriate parameters using the following code:

```python
model = FastText(
            vocab_size = len(vocab),
            embedding_dim = 100,
```

```
                    output_dim = 1,
                    pad_idx = vocab['<PAD>'])
```

Rather than train our embedding layer from scratch, we'll initialize the layer's weights with pretrained embeddings. This process is similar to how we used pretrained weights in the transfer learning example in "Image Classification with Transfer Learning" on page 104:

```
pretrained_embeddings = vocab.vectors  ❶
model.embedding.weight.data.copy_(
                    pretrained_embeddings)  ❷

EMBEDDING_DIM = 100
unk_idx = vocab['<UNK>']  ❸
pad_idx = vocab['<PAD>']
model.embedding.weight.data[unk_idx] = \
      torch.zeros(EMBEDDING_DIM)          ❹
model.embedding.weight.data[pad_idx] = \
      torch.zeros(EMBEDDING_DIM)
```

❶ Load the pretrained embedding from our vocabulary.

❷ Initialize the embedding layer's weights.

❸ Initialize the embedding weights of an unknown token to zero.

❹ Initialize the embedding weights of a pad token to zero.

Now that it's initialized properly, we can train our model.

Training and Validation

The training and validation process should look familiar. It's similar to the one we've used in previous examples. First we configure our loss function and our optimizer algorithm, as shown in the following code:

```
import torch.optim as optim

optimizer = optim.Adam(model.parameters())
criterion = nn.BCEWithLogitsLoss()
```

```
model = model.to(device)
criterion = criterion.to(device)
```

In this example, we are using the Adam optimizer and the BCE WithLogitsLoss() loss function. The Adam optimizer is a replacement for SGD and performs better for sparse or noisy gradients. The BCEWithLogitsLoss() function is commonly used for binary classification. We also move our model to a GPU if available.

Next we run our training and validation loops, as shown in the following code:

```python
for epoch in range(5):
    epoch_loss = 0
    epoch_acc = 0

    model.train()
    for label, text, _ in train_dataloader:
        optimizer.zero_grad()
        predictions = model(text).squeeze(1)
        loss = criterion(predictions, label)

        rounded_preds = torch.round(
            torch.sigmoid(predictions))
        correct = \
          (rounded_preds == label).float()
        acc = correct.sum() / len(correct)

        loss.backward()
        optimizer.step()
        epoch_loss += loss.item()
        epoch_acc += acc.item()

    print("Epoch %d Train: Loss: %.4f Acc: %.4f" %
          (epoch,
           epoch_loss / len(train_dataloader),
           epoch_acc / len(train_dataloader)))

    epoch_loss = 0
    epoch_acc = 0
    model.eval()
    with torch.no_grad():
      for label, text, _ in valid_dataloader:
        predictions = model(text).squeeze(1)
        loss = criterion(predictions, label)

        rounded_preds = torch.round(
```

```
        torch.sigmoid(predictions))
    correct = \
      (rounded_preds == label).float()
    acc = correct.sum() / len(correct)

    epoch_loss += loss.item()
    epoch_acc += acc.item()

  print("Epoch %d Valid: Loss: %.4f Acc: %.4f" %
        (epoch,
         epoch_loss / len(valid_dataloader),
         epoch_acc / len(valid_dataloader)))

# out: (your results may vary)
# Epoch 0 Train: Loss: 0.6523 Acc: 0.7165
# Epoch 0 Valid: Loss: 0.5259 Acc: 0.7474
# Epoch 1 Train: Loss: 0.5935 Acc: 0.7765
# Epoch 1 Valid: Loss: 0.4571 Acc: 0.7933
# Epoch 2 Train: Loss: 0.5230 Acc: 0.8257
# Epoch 2 Valid: Loss: 0.4103 Acc: 0.8245
# Epoch 3 Train: Loss: 0.4559 Acc: 0.8598
# Epoch 3 Valid: Loss: 0.3828 Acc: 0.8549
# Epoch 4 Train: Loss: 0.4004 Acc: 0.8813
# Epoch 4 Valid: Loss: 0.3781 Acc: 0.8675
```

We should see validation accuracies around 85–90% with only five epochs of training. Let's see how our model performs against the test dataset.

Testing and Deployment

Earlier, we constructed our `test_iterator` based on the IMDb test dataset. Recall that none of the data in the test dataset has been used for training or validation.

Our test loop is shown in the following code:

```
test_loss = 0
test_acc = 0
model.eval() ❶
with torch.no_grad(): ❶
  for label, text, _ in test_dataloader:
    predictions = model(text).squeeze(1)
    loss = criterion(predictions, label)

    rounded_preds = torch.round(
        torch.sigmoid(predictions))
```

```
        correct = \
          (rounded_preds == label).float()
        acc = correct.sum() / len(correct)

        test_loss += loss.item()
        test_acc += acc.item()

print("Test: Loss: %.4f Acc: %.4f" %
        (test_loss / len(test_dataloader),
         test_acc / len(test_dataloader)))
# out: (your results will vary)
#   Test: Loss: 0.3821 Acc: 0.8599
```

❶ Not necessary for this model, but good practice.

In the preceding code, we process one batch at a time and cumulate the accuracy over the entire test dataset. You should get 85–90% accuracy on the test set as well.

Next we'll predict the sentiment of our own reviews, using the following code:

```
import spacy
nlp = spacy.load('en_core_web_sm')

def predict_sentiment(model, sentence):
    model.eval()
    text = torch.tensor(text_pipeline(
      sentence)).unsqueeze(1).to(device)
    prediction = torch.sigmoid(model(text))
    return prediction.item()

sentiment = predict_sentiment(model,
                "Don't waste your time")
print(sentiment)
# out: 4.763594888613835e-34

sentiment = predict_sentiment(model,
                "You gotta see this movie!")
print(sentiment)
# out: 0.941755473613739
```

A result close to 0 corresponds to a negative review, while an output close to 1 indicates a positive review. As you can see, the model correctly predicted the sentiment of the sample review. Try it with some of your own movie reviews!

Finally, we'll save our model for deployment as shown in the following code:

```
torch.save(model.state_dict(), 'fasttext-model.pt')
```

In this example, you learned how to preprocess text data and designed a FastText model for sentiment analysis. You also trained the model, evaluated its performance, and saved the model for deployment. You can use this design pattern and reference code to solve other sentiment analysis problems in your own work.

This example was based on the "Faster Sentiment Analysis" tutorial by Ben Trevett. You can find more details and other great Torchtext tutorials in his PyTorch Sentiment Analysis GitHub repository (*https://pytorch.tips/sentiment-tutorials*).

Let's move on to our final reference design, in which we will use deep learning and PyTorch to generate image data.

Generative Learning—Generating Fashion-MNIST Images with DCGAN

One of the most interesting areas of deep learning is *generative learning*, in which NNs are used to create data. Sometimes these NNs can create images, music, text, and time series data so well that it is difficult to tell the difference between real data and the generated data. Generative learning is used to create images of people and places that don't exist, increase image resolution, predict frames in video, augment datasets, generate news articles, and convert styles of art and music.

In this section, I'll show you how to use PyTorch for generative learning. The development process is similar to the previous examples; however, here we'll use an unsupervised approach in which the data is not labeled.

In addition, we'll design and train a GAN, which is quite different from the models and training loops of previous examples. Testing and evaluating the GAN involves a slightly different process as well. The overall development sequence is consistent with the process in Chapter 2, but each part will be unique to generative learning.

In this example, we will train a GAN to generate images similar to the training images used in the Fashion-MNIST dataset. Fashion-MNIST is a popular academic dataset used for image classification that includes images of articles of clothing. Let's access the Fashion-MNIST data to get an idea of what these images look like, and then we'll create some synthetic images based on what we've seen.

Data Processing

Unlike models used for supervised learning, where the model learns the relationships between data and labels, generative models look to learn the distribution of the training data so as to generate data similar to the training data at hand. Therefore, in this example we only need training data, because if we build a good model and train it long enough, the model should begin to produce good synthetic data.

First let's import the required libraries, define some constants, and set our device:

```
import torch
from torch.utils.data import DataLoader
from torchvision import datasets, transforms

CODING_SIZE = 100
BATCH_SIZE = 32
IMAGE_SIZE = 64

device = torch.device("cuda:0" if
  torch.cuda.is_available() else "cpu")
```

The following code loads the training data, defines the transforms, and creates a dataloader for batch iteration:

```
transform = transforms.Compose([
    transforms.Resize(IMAGE_SIZE),
    transforms.ToTensor(),
])
```

```
dataset = datasets.FashionMNIST(
              './',
              train=True,
              download=True,
              transform=transform)

dataloader = DataLoader(
              dataset,
              batch_size=BATCH_SIZE,
              shuffle=True,
              num_workers=8)
```

This code should look familiar to you. We are once again using
Torchvision functions to define the transforms, create a dataset,
and set up a dataloader that will sample the dataset, apply
transforms, and return a batch of images for our model.

We can display a batch of images with the following code:

```
from torchvision.utils import make_grid
import matplotlib.pyplot as plt

data_batch, labels_batch = next(iter(dataloader))
grid_img = make_grid(data_batch, nrow=8)
plt.imshow(grid_img.permute(1, 2, 0))
```

Torchvision provides a nice utility called make_grid to display a
grid of images. Figure 4-2 shows an example batch of Fashion-
MNIST images.

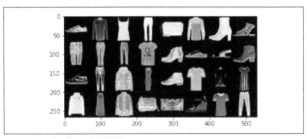

Figure 4-2. Fashion-MNIST images

Let's see what model we'll use for our data generation task.

Model Design

To generate new image data, we'll use a GAN. The goal of the GAN model is to generate "fake" data based on the training data's distribution. The GAN accomplishes this goal with two distinct modules: the generator and the discriminator.

The job of the generator is to generate fake images that look real. The job of the discriminator is to correctly identify whether an image is fake. Although the design of GANs is beyond the scope of this book, I'll provide a sample reference design using a deep convolutional GAN, or DCGAN.

NOTE

GANs were first described in the famous paper by Ian Goodfellow et al. in 2014 titled "Generative Adversarial Nets" (*https://pytorch.tips/gan-paper*). Guidelines for building more stable convolutional GANs were proposed by Alec Radford et al. in the 2015 paper "Unsupervised Representation Learning with Deep Convolutional Generative Adversarial Networks" (*https://pytorch.tips/dcgan-paper*). This paper describes the DCGAN used in this example.

The generator is designed to create an image from an input vector of 100 random values. Here's the code:

```
import torch.nn as nn

class Generator(nn.Module):
    def __init__(self, coding_sz):
        super(Generator, self).__init__()
        self.net = nn.Sequential(
            nn.ConvTranspose2d(coding_sz,
                                1024, 4, 1, 0),
            nn.BatchNorm2d(1024),
            nn.ReLU(),
            nn.ConvTranspose2d(1024,
                                512, 4, 2, 1),
            nn.BatchNorm2d(512),
            nn.ReLU(),
```

```
            nn.ConvTranspose2d(512,
                               256, 4, 2, 1),
            nn.BatchNorm2d(256),
            nn.ReLU(),
            nn.ConvTranspose2d(256,
                               128, 4, 2, 1),
            nn.BatchNorm2d(128),
            nn.ReLU(),
            nn.ConvTranspose2d(128,
                               1, 4, 2, 1),
            nn.Tanh()
        )

    def forward(self, input):
        return self.net(input)

netG = Generator(CODING_SIZE).to(device)
```

This example generator uses 2D convolutional transpose layers with batch normalization and ReLU activations. The layers are defined in the __init__() function. It works like our image classification models, except in reverse order.

That is, instead of reducing an image to a smaller representation, it takes a random vector and creates a full image from it. We also instantiate the Generator module as netG.

Next, we create the Discriminator module, as shown in the following code:

```
class Discriminator(nn.Module):
    def __init__(self):
        super(Discriminator,
              self).__init__()
        self.net = nn.Sequential(
            nn.Conv2d(1, 128, 4, 2, 1),
            nn.LeakyReLU(0.2),
            nn.Conv2d(128, 256, 4, 2, 1),
            nn.BatchNorm2d(256),
            nn.LeakyReLU(0.2),
            nn.Conv2d(256, 512, 4, 2, 1),
            nn.BatchNorm2d(512),
            nn.LeakyReLU(0.2),
            nn.Conv2d(512, 1024, 4, 2, 1),
            nn.BatchNorm2d(1024),
            nn.LeakyReLU(0.2),
            nn.Conv2d(1024, 1, 4, 1, 0),
            nn.Sigmoid()
```

```
        )

    def forward(self, input):
        return self.net(input)

netD = Discriminator().to(device)
```

The discriminator is a binary classification network that determines the probability that the input image is real. This example discriminator NN uses 2D convolutional layers with batch normalization and leaky ReLU activation functions. We instantiate the Discriminator as netD.

The authors of the DCGAN paper found that it helps to initialize the weights as shown in the following code:

```
def weights_init(m):
    classname = m.__class__.__name__
    if classname.find('Conv') != -1:
        nn.init.normal_(m.weight.data, 0.0, 0.02)
    elif classname.find('BatchNorm') != -1:
        nn.init.normal_(m.weight.data, 1.0, 0.02)
        nn.init.constant_(m.bias.data, 0)

netG.apply(weights_init)
netD.apply(weights_init)
```

Now that we have designed our two modules, we can set up and train the GAN.

Training

Training a GAN is somewhat more complicated than the previous training examples. In each epoch, we will first train the discriminator with a real batch of data, then use the generator to create a fake batch, and then train the discriminator with the generated fake batch of data. Lastly, we will train the generator NN to produce better fakes.

This is a good example of how powerful PyTorch is when creating custom training loops. It provides the flexibility to develop and implement new ideas with ease.

Before we start training, we need to define the loss function and optimizers that will be used to train the generator and the discriminator:

```
from torch import optim

criterion = nn.BCELoss()

optimizerG = optim.Adam(netG.parameters(),
                        lr=0.0002,
                        betas=(0.5, 0.999))
optimizerD = optim.Adam(netD.parameters(),
                        lr=0.0001,
                        betas=(0.5, 0.999))
```

In the preceding code, we define a label for real versus fake images. Then we use the binary cross entropy (BCE) loss function, which is commonly used for binary classification. Remember the discriminator is performing binary classification by classifying an image as real or fake. We use the commonly used Adam optimizer for updating the model parameters.

Let's define values for the real and fake labels and create tensors for computing the loss:

```
real_labels = torch.full((BATCH_SIZE,),
                         1.,
                         dtype=torch.float,
                         device=device)

fake_labels = torch.full((BATCH_SIZE,),
                         0.,
                         dtype=torch.float,
                         device=device)
```

Before we start training, we will create lists for storing the errors and define a test vector to show the results later:

```
G_losses = []
D_losses = []
D_real = []
D_fake = []

z = torch.randn((
    BATCH_SIZE, 100)).view(-1, 100, 1, 1).to(device)
test_out_images = []
```

Now we can execute the training loop. If the GAN is stable, it should improve as more epochs are trained. The training loop is shown in the following code:

```
N_EPOCHS = 5

for epoch in range(N_EPOCHS):
  print(f'Epoch: {epoch}')
  for i, batch in enumerate(dataloader):
    if (i%200==0):
      print(f'batch: {i} of {len(dataloader)}')

    # Train Discriminator with an all-real batch.
    netD.zero_grad()
    real_images = batch[0].to(device) *2. - 1.
    output = netD(real_images).view(-1)  ❶
    errD_real = criterion(output, real_labels)
    D_x = output.mean().item()

    # Train Discriminator with an all-fake batch.
    noise = torch.randn((BATCH_SIZE,
                         CODING_SIZE))
    noise = noise.view(-1,100,1,1).to(device)
    fake_images = netG(noise)
    output = netD(fake_images).view(-1)  ❷
    errD_fake = criterion(output, fake_labels)
    D_G_z1 = output.mean().item()
    errD = errD_real + errD_fake
    errD.backward(retain_graph=True)  ❸
    optimizerD.step()

    # Train Generator to generate better fakes.
    netG.zero_grad()
    output = netD(fake_images).view(-1)  ❹
    errG = criterion(output, real_labels)  ❺
    errG.backward()  ❻
    D_G_z2 = output.mean().item()
    optimizerG.step()

    # Save losses for plotting later.
    G_losses.append(errG.item())
    D_losses.append(errD.item())

    D_real.append(D_x)
    D_fake.append(D_G_z2)
```

```
test_images = netG(z).to('cpu').detach() ❼
test_out_images.append(test_images)
```

❶ Pass real images to the Discriminator.

❷ Pass fake images to the Discriminator.

❸ Run backpropagation and update the Discriminator.

❹ Pass fake images to the updated Discriminator.

❺ The Generator loss is based on cases in which the[.keep-together] Discriminator is wrong.

❻ Run backpropagation and update the Generator.

❼ Create a batch of images and save them after each epoch.

As we've done in the previous examples, we loop through all the data, one batch at a time, using the dataloader during each epoch. First we train the discriminator with a batch of real images so it can compute the output, calculate the loss, and compute the gradients. Then we train the discriminator with a batch of fake images.

The fake images are created by the generator from a vector of random values. Again, we compute the discriminator output, calculate the loss, and compute the gradients. Next, we add the gradients from all the real and all the fake batches and apply backpropagation.

We compute the outputs from the freshly trained discriminator using the same fake data, and compute the loss or error of the generator. Using this loss, we compute the gradients and apply backpropagation on the generator itself.

Lastly, we'll keep track of the loss after each epoch to see if the GAN's training is consistently improving and stable. Figure 4-3 shows the loss curve for both the generator and the discriminator during training.

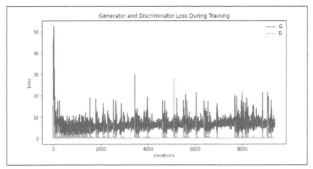

Figure 4-3. GAN training curves

The loss curves plot the generator and the discriminator loss for each batch over all epochs, so the loss bounces around depending on the computed loss of the batch. We can see though that the loss in both cases has been reduced from the beginning of training. If we trained over more epochs, we'd look for these loss values to approach zero.

In general, GANs are tricky to train, and the learning rate, betas, and other optimizer hyperparameters can have a major impact.

Let's examine the average results of the discriminator for each batch over all the epochs, as shown in Figure 4-4.

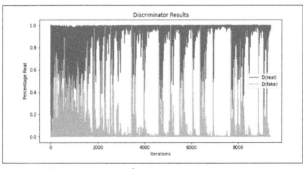

Figure 4-4. Discriminator results

If the GAN was perfect, the discriminator would not be able to correctly identify fake images as fake or real images as real, and we would expect the average error to be 0.5 in both cases. The results show that some batches are close to 0.5, but we can certainly do better.

Now that we have trained our network, let's see how well it does at creating fake images of clothing.

Testing and Deployment

During supervised learning, we usually set aside a test dataset that has not been used to train or validate the model. In generative learning, there are no labels produced by the generator. We could pass our generated images into a Fashion-MNIST classifier, but there's no way for us to know if the errors are caused by the classifier or the GAN unless we hand-label the outputs.

For now, let's test and evaluate our GAN by comparing the results from the first epoch with the generated images from the last epoch. We create a test vector, z, for testing and use the computed generator results at the end of each epoch in our training loop code.

Figure 4-5 shows the generated images from the first epoch, while Figure 4-6 shows the results after training only five epochs.

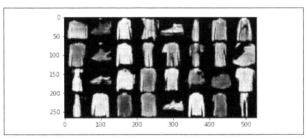

Figure 4-5. Generator results (first epoch)

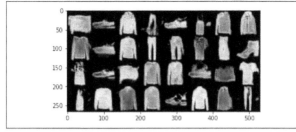

Figure 4-6. Generator results (last epoch)

You can see that the generator has improved some. Look at the boot at the end of the second row or the shirt at the end of the third row. Our GAN is not perfect, but it seems to be improving after just five epochs. Training over more epochs or improving our design might produce even better results.

Finally, we can save our trained model for deployment and use it to generate more synthetic Fashion-MNIST images using the following code:

```
torch.save(netG.state_dict(), './gan.pt')
```

We expanded our PyTorch deep learning capabilities by designing and training a GAN in this generative learning reference design. You can use this reference design to create and train other GAN models and test their performance at generating new data.

In this chapter, we covered additional examples to show a variety of data processing, model design, and training approaches with PyTorch—but what if you have an amazing idea for some new, innovative NN? Or what if you come up with a new optimization algorithm or loss function that nobody's seen before? In the next chapter, I'll show you how to create your own custom modules and functions so you can expand your deep learning research and experiment with new ideas.

## CHAPTER 5

Customizing PyTorch

Up until now, you have been using built-in PyTorch classes, functions, and libraries to design and train various predefined models, model layers, and activation functions. But what if you have a novel idea or you're conducting cutting-edge deep learning research? Perhaps you've invented a totally new layer architecture or activation function. Maybe you've developed a new optimization algorithm or a special loss function that no one's ever seen before.

In this chapter, I'll show you how to create your own custom deep learning components and algorithms in PyTorch. We'll begin by exploring how to create custom layers and activation functions, and then we'll see how to combine these components into custom model architectures. Next, I'll show you how to create your own loss functions and optimizer algorithms. Finally, we'll look at how to create custom loops for training, validation, and testing.

PyTorch offers flexibility: you can extend an existing library or you can combine your customizations into your own library or package. By creating custom components you can solve new deep learning problems, speed up training, and discover innovative ways to perform deep learning.

Let's get started by creating some custom deep learning layers and activation functions.

Custom Layers and Activations

PyTorch offers an extensive set of built-in layers and activation functions. However, what makes PyTorch so popular, especially in the research community, is how easy it is to create custom layers and activations. The ability to do so can facilitate experimentation and accelerate your research.

If we take a look at the PyTorch source code, we'll see that layers and activations are created using a functional definition and a class implementation. The *functional definition* specifies how the outputs are created based on the inputs. It is defined in the nn.functional module. The *class implementation* is used to create an object that calls this function at its core, but it also includes added features derived from the nn.Module class.

For example, let's look at how the fully connected nn.Linear layer is implemented. The following code shows a simplified version of the functional definition, nn.functional.linear():

```
import torch

def linear(input, weight, bias=None):

    if input.dim() == 2 and bias is not None:
        # fused op is marginally faster
        ret = torch.addmm(bias, input, weight.t())
    else:
        output = input.matmul(weight.t())
        if bias is not None:
            output += bias
        ret = output
    return ret
```

The linear() function multiplies the input tensor by the weight matrix, optionally adds the bias vector, and returns the results in a tensor. You can see that the code is optimized for performance. When the input has two dimensions and there is no bias, you should use the fused-matrix add function, torch.addmm(), because it's faster in this case.

Keeping the mathematical computations in a separate functional definition has the benefit of keeping optimizations separate from the layer nn.Module. The functional definitions can also be used as standalone functions when writing code in general.

However, we'll often use the nn.Module class to subclass our NNs. When we create an nn.Module subclass, we gain all the built-in benefits of the nn.Module object. In this case, we derive the nn.Linear class from nn.Module, as shown in the following code:

```python
import torch.nn as nn
from torch import Tensor

class Linear(nn.Module):

    def __init__(self, in_features,
                 out_features, bias):      ❶
        super(Linear, self).__init__()
        self.in_features = in_features
        self.out_features = out_features
        self.weight = Parameter(
            torch.Tensor(out_features,
                         in_features))
        if bias:
            self.bias = Parameter(
                torch.Tensor(out_features))
        else:
            self.register_parameter('bias', None)
        self.reset_parameters()

    def reset_parameters(self):
        init.kaiming_uniform_(self.weight,
                              a=math.sqrt(5))
        if self.bias is not None:
            fan_in, _ = \
              init._calculate_fan_in_and_fan_out(
                self.weight)
            bound = 1 / math.sqrt(fan_in)
            init.uniform_(self.bias, -bound, bound)

    def forward(self, input: Tensor) -> Tensor:  ❷
        return F.linear(input,
                        self.weight,
                        self.bias)  ❸
```

❶ Initialize input and output sizes, weights, and biases.

❷ Define the forward pass.

❸ Use the functional definition of `linear()`.

The `nn.Linear` code includes two necessary methods for any `nn.Module` subclass. One is `__init__()`, which initializes the class attributes, namely the inputs, outputs, weights, and biases in this case. The other is the `forward()` method, which defines the processing during the forward pass.

As you can see in the preceding code, the `forward()` method often calls the `nn.functional` definition associated with the layer. This convention is used often in PyTorch code for layers.

The convention for creating a custom layer is to first create a function that implements the mathematical operations and then create an `nn.Module` subclass that uses this function to implement the layer class. Using this approach makes it very easy to experiment with new layer designs in your PyTorch model development.

Custom Layer Example (Complex Linear)

Next, we'll look at how to create a custom layer. In this example, we will create our own linear layer for a special type of number called a *complex number*. Complex numbers are often used in physics and signal processing and consist of a pair of numbers—a "real" component and an "imaginary" component. Both components are just floating-point numbers.

PyTorch is adding support for complex data types; however, they are still in beta at the time of writing of this book. Therefore, we'll implement them using two floating-point tensors, one for the real components and one for the imaginary components.

In this case, the inputs, weights, biases, and outputs will all be complex numbers and will consist of two tensors instead of one. Complex multiplication yields the following equation (where j is the complex number $\sqrt{1}$):

$$\left(in_r + in_i{}^* j\right){}^* \left(w_r + w_i{}^* j\right) + \left(b_r + b_i{}^* j\right)$$
$$= \left(in_r{}^* w_r - in_i{}^* w_i + b_r\right) + \left(in_r{}^* w_i + in_i{}^* w_r + b_i\right){}^* j$$

First we will create a functional version of our complex linear layer, as shown in the following code:

```
def complex_linear(in_r, in_i, w_r, w_i, b_i, b_r):
    out_r = (in_r.matmul(w_r.t())
            - in_i.matmul(w_i.t()) + b_r)
    out_i = (in_r.matmul(w_i.t())
            - in_i.matmul(w_r.t()) + b_i)

    return out_r, out_i
```

As you can see, the function applies the complex multiplication formula to tensor arrays. Next we create our class version of ComplexLinear based on the nn.Module, as shown in the following code:

```
class ComplexLinear(nn.Module):
    def __init__(self, in_features, out_features):
        super(Linear, self).__init__()
        self.in_features = in_features
        self.out_features = out_features
        self.weight_r = \
          Parameter(torch.randn(out_features,
                                in_features))
        self.weight_i = \
          Parameter(torch.randn(out_features,
                                in_features))
        self.bias_r = Parameter(
                        torch.randn(out_features))
        self.bias_i = Parameter(
                        torch.randn(out_features))

    def forward(self, in_r, in_i):
        return F.complex_linear(in_r, in_i,
                self.weight_r, self.weight_i,
                self.bias_r, self.bias_i)
```

In our class, we define separate weights and biases for the real and imaginary components in our __init__() function. Note that the options for the number of in_features and out_fea tures do not change because the number of real and imaginary components are the same. Our forward() function simply calls the functional definition of our complex multiply and add operation.

Note that we could also use PyTorch's existing nn.Linear layer to build our layer, as shown in the following code:

```
class ComplexLinearSimple(nn.Module):
    def __init__(self, in_features, out_features):
        super(ComplexLinearSimple, self).__init__()
        self.fc_r = Linear(in_features,
                           out_features)
        self.fc_i = Linear(in_features,
                           out_features)

    def forward(self,in_r, in_i):
        return (self.fc_r(in_r) - self.fc_i(in_i),
                self.fc_r(in_i)+self.fc_i(in_r))
```

In this code, we get all the added benefits from nn.Linear for free, and we do not need to implement a new functional definition. When you create your own custom layers, check PyTorch's built-in layers to see if you can reuse existing classes.

Even though this example was pretty simple, you can use the same approach to create more complex layers. In addition, the same approach can also be used to create custom activation functions.

Activation functions are very similar to NN layers in that they return outputs by performing mathematical operations on a set of inputs. They differ in that the operations are performed element-wise, and they do not include parameters like weights and biases that are adjusted during training. For this reason, activation functions can be performed solely with functional versions.

For example, let's take a look at the ReLU activation function. The ReLU function is zero for negative values and linear for positive values:

```python
def my_relu(input, thresh=0.0):
    return torch.where(
                input > thresh,
                input,
                torch.zeros_like(input))
```

When the activation function has configurable parameters, it's common to create a class version of it. We can add the capability to adjust the threshold and value of the ReLU function by creating a ReLU class, as shown in the following code:

```python
class MyReLU(nn.Module):
    def __init__(self, thresh = 0.0):
        super(MyReLU, self).__init__()
        self.thresh = thresh

    def forward(self, input):
        return my_relu(input, self.thresh)
```

When building an NN, it is common to use the functional version of the activation function, but a class version can also be used if available. The following code snippets show how to use both versions of the ReLU activation included in torch.nn.

Here's the functional version:

```python
import torch.nn.functional as F  ❶

class SimpleNet(nn.Module):
    def __init__(self, D_in, H, D_out):
        super(SimpleNet, self).__init__()
        self.fc1 = nn.Linear(D_in, H)
        self.fc2 = nn.Linear(H, D_out)

    def forward(self, x):
        x = F.relu(self.fc1(x))  ❷
        return self.fc2(x)
```

❶ A common way to import the functional package.

❷ The functional version of ReLU is used here.

Here's the class version:

```
class SimpleNet(nn.Module):
  def __init__(self, D_in, H, D_out):
    super(SimpleNet, self).__init__()
    self.net = nn.Sequential( ❶
        nn.Linear(D_in, H),
        nn.ReLU(), ❷
        nn.Linear(H, D_out)
    )

  def forward(self, x):
    return self.net(x)
```

❶ We are using nn.Sequential() since all components are classes.

❷ We are using the class version of ReLU.

Custom Activation Example (Complex ReLU)

We can create our own custom ComplexReLU activation function to handle complex values from the ComplexLinear layer that we created earlier. The following code shows the functional and class versions:

```
def complex_relu(in_r, in_i): ❶
    return (F.relu(in_r), F.relu(in_i))

class ComplexReLU(nn.Module): ❷
  def __init__(self):
      super(ComplexReLU, self).__init__()

  def forward(self, in_r, in_i):
      return complex_relu(in_r, in_i)
```

❶ Functional version

❷ Class version

Now that you've learned how to create your own layers and activations, let's see how you can create your own custom model architectures.

Custom Model Architectures

In Chapters 2 and 3, we used built-in models and created our own models from built-in PyTorch layers. In this section, we'll explore how you can create a library of models similar to torchvision.models and build flexible model classes that adjust the architecture based on configuration parameters provided by the user.

The torchvision.models package provides an AlexNet model class and an alexnet() convenience function to facilitate its use. Let's look at the AlexNet class first:

```python
class AlexNet(nn.Module):

    def __init__(self, num_classes=1000):
        super(AlexNet, self).__init__()
        self.features = nn.Sequential(
            nn.Conv2d(3, 64, kernel_size=11,
                        stride=4, padding=2),
            nn.ReLU(inplace=True),
            nn.MaxPool2d(kernel_size=3, stride=2),
            nn.Conv2d(64, 192, kernel_size=5,
                        padding=2),
            nn.ReLU(inplace=True),
            nn.MaxPool2d(kernel_size=3, stride=2),
            nn.Conv2d(192, 384, kernel_size=3,
                        padding=1),
            nn.ReLU(inplace=True),
            nn.Conv2d(384, 256, kernel_size=3,
                        padding=1),
            nn.ReLU(inplace=True),
            nn.Conv2d(256, 256, kernel_size=3,
                        padding=1),
            nn.ReLU(inplace=True),
            nn.MaxPool2d(kernel_size=3, stride=2),
        )
        self.avgpool = nn.AdaptiveAvgPool2d((6, 6))
        self.classifier = nn.Sequential(
            nn.Dropout(),
            nn.Linear(256 * 6 * 6, 4096),
            nn.ReLU(inplace=True),
            nn.Dropout(),
            nn.Linear(4096, 4096),
            nn.ReLU(inplace=True),
            nn.Linear(4096, num_classes),
        )
```

```
def forward(self, x):
    x = self.features(x)
    x = self.avgpool(x)
    x = torch.flatten(x, 1)
    x = self.classifier(x)
    return x
```

Like all layers, activations, and models, the AlexNet class is derived from the nn.Module class. The AlexNet class is a good example of how to create and combine submodules into an NN.

The library defines three subnetworks—features, avgpool, and classifier. Each subnetwork is made up of PyTorch layers and activations, and they are connected in sequence. AlexNet's forward() function describes the forward pass; that is, how the inputs are processed to form the outputs.

In this case, the PyTorch torchvision.models code provides a convenience function called alexnet() to instantiate or create the model with some options. The options here are pretrained and progress; they determine whether to load the model with pretrained parameters and whether to display a progress bar:

```
from torch.hub import load_state_dict_from_url
model_urls = {
    'alexnet':
    'https://pytorch.tips/alexnet-download',
}

def alexnet(pretrained=False,
            progress=True, **kwargs):
    model = AlexNet(**kwargs)
    if pretrained:
        state_dict = load_state_dict_from_url(
            model_urls['alexnet'],
            progress=progress)
        model.load_state_dict(state_dict)
    return model
```

The **kwargs parameter allows you to pass additional options to the AlexNet model. In this case, you can change the number of classes to 10 with alexnet(n_classes = 10). The function will instantiate the AlexNet model with n_classes = 10 and return the model object. If `pretrained` is `True`, the function will load the weights from the specified URL.

By following a similar approach, you can create your own model architectures. Create a top-level model that is derived from `nn.Module`. Define your `__init__()` and `forward()` functions and implement your NN based on subnetworks, layers, and activations. Your subnetworks, layers, and activations can even be custom ones that you created yourself.

As you can see, the `nn.Module` class makes creating custom models easy. In addition to the `Module` class, the `torch.nn` package includes built-in loss functions. Let's take a look at how you can create your own loss functions.

Custom Loss Functions

If you recall from Chapter 3, before we can train our NN model, we need to define our loss function. The loss function, or cost function, defines a metric which we wish to minimize by adjusting the weights of our model during training.

At first it might appear that the loss function is just a functional definition, but remember, the loss function is a function of the parameters of the NN module.

Therefore, loss functions actually behave like an extra layer that takes the NN outputs as inputs and produces a metric as its output. When we perform backpropagation, we're performing backpropagation on the loss function, not the NN.

This allows us to call the class directly to compute the loss given the NN outputs and true values. Then we can compute the gradients of all the NN parameters in one call, namely to perform backpropagation. The following code shows how this can be implemented in code:

```
loss_fcn = nn.MSELoss()  ❶
loss = loss_fcn(outputs, targets)
loss.backward()
```

❶ Sometimes called `criterion`

First we instantiate the loss function, itself and then we call the function passing in the outputs (from our model) and the targets (from our data). Finally, we call the `backward()` method to perform backpropagation and compute the gradients of all the model parameters with respect to the loss.

Similar to layers discussed earlier, loss functions are implemented using a functional definition and a class implementation derived from the `nn.Module` class.

Simplified versions of the functional definition and the class implementations for `mse_loss` are shown in the following code:

```python
def mse_loss(input, target):
    return ((input-target)**2).mean()

class MSELoss(nn.Module):
    def __init__(self):
        super(MSELoss, self).__init__()

    def forward(self, input, target):
        return F.mse_loss(input, target)
```

Let's create our own loss function, MSE Loss for Complex Numbers. To create our own custom loss function, we'll first define a functional definition that describes the loss function mathematically. Then we'll create the loss function class, as shown in the following code:

```python
def complex_mse_loss(input_r, input_i,
                     target_r, target_i):
    return (((input_r-target_r)**2).mean(),
            ((input_i-target_i)**2).mean())

class ComplexMSELoss(nn.Module):
    def __init__(self, real_only=False):
        super(ComplexMSELoss, self).__init__()
        self.real_only = real_only

    def forward(self, input_r, input_i,
                target_r, target_i):
        if (self.real_only):
            return F.mse_loss(input_r, target_r)
        else:
```

```
        return complex_mse_loss(
            input_r, input_i,
            target_r, target_i)
```

This time, we created an optional setting in the class called
`real_only`. When we instantiate the loss function with
`real_only = True`, the functional `mse_loss()` will be used
instead of `complex_mse_loss()`.

As you can see, PyTorch offers exceptional flexibility in building custom model architectures and loss functions. Before we
get to training, there's one more function you can customize:
the optimizer. Let's see how you can create custom optimizers.

Custom Optimizer Algorithms

The optimizer plays an important part in training your NN
model. An optimizer is an algorithm that updates the model's
parameters during training. When we perform backpropagation using `loss.backward()`, we determine whether the parameters should be increased or decreased to minimize the loss.
The optimizer uses the gradients to determine how much the
parameters should be changed during each step and changes
them.

PyTorch has its own submodule called `torch.optim` that contains many built-in optimizer algorithms, as we saw in Chapter 3. To create an optimizer, we pass in our model's parameters
and any optimizer-specific options. For example, the following
code creates an SGD optimizer with a learning rate of 0.01 and
momentum value of 0.9:

```
from torch import optim

optimizer = optim.SGD(model.parameters(),
                      lr=0.01, momentum=0.9)
```

In PyTorch we can also specify different options for different
parameters. This is useful when you want to specify different
learning rates for the different layers of your model. Each set of
parameters is called a parameter group. We can specify different options using dictionaries, as shown in the following code:

```
optim.SGD([
        {'params':
          model.features.parameters()},
        {'params':
          model.classifier.parameters(),
          'lr': 1e-3}
    ], lr=1e-2, momentum=0.9)
```

Assuming we are using the AlexNet model, the preceding code sets the learning rate to 1e-3 for the classifier layer and uses the default learning rate of 1e-2 for the features layer.

PyTorch provides a `torch.optim.Optimizer` base class to make it easy to create your own custom optimizers. Here is a simplified version of the `Optimizer` base class:

```
from collections import defaultdict

class Optimizer(object):

    def __init__(self, params, defaults):
        self.defaults = defaults
        self.state = defaultdict(dict)  ❶
        self.param_groups = []  ❷

        param_groups = list(params)
        if len(param_groups) == 0:
            raise ValueError(
                """optimizer got an
                empty parameter list""")
        if not isinstance(param_groups[0], dict):
            param_groups = [{'params': param_groups}]

        for param_group in param_groups:
            self.add_param_group(param_group)

    def __getstate__(self):
        return {
            'defaults': self.defaults,
            'state': self.state,
            'param_groups': self.param_groups,
        }

    def __setstate__(self, state):
        self.__dict__.update(state)

    def zero_grad(self):  ❸
```

```
for group in self.param_groups:
    for p in group['params']:
        if p.grad is not None:
            p.grad.detach_()
            p.grad.zero_()

def step(self, closure): ❹
    raise NotImplementedError
```

❶ Define state as needed.

❷ Define param_groups as needed.

❸ Define zero_grad() as needed.

❹ You'll need to write your own step().

There are two main attributes or components to the optimizer: state and param_groups. The state atribute is a dictionary that can vary across different optimizers. It is mainly used to maintain values between each call to the step() function. The param_groups attribute is also a dictionary. It contains the parameters themselves and the associated options for each group.

The important methods in the Optimizer base class are zero_grad() and step(). The zero_grad() method is used to zero or reset the gradients during each training iteration. The step() method is used to execute the optimizer algorithm, compute the change for each parameter, and update the parameters within the model object. The zero_grad() method is already implemented for you. However, you must create your own step() method when creating your custom optimizer.

Let's demonstrate the process by creating our own simple version of SGD. Our SDG optimizer will have one option—the learning rate (LR). During each optimizer step we will multiply the gradient by the LR and add it to the parameter (i.e., adjust the model's weights):

```
from torch.optim import Optimizer

class SimpleSGD(Optimizer):

    def __init__(self, params, lr='required'):
        if lr is not 'required' and lr < 0.0:
          raise ValueError(
            "Invalid learning rate: {}".format(lr))

        defaults = dict(lr=lr)
        super(SimpleSGD, self).__init__(
            params, defaults)

    def step(self):
        for group in self.param_groups:
            for p in group['params']:
                if p.grad is None:
                    continue
                d_p = p.grad
                p.add_(d_p, alpha=-group['lr'])

        return
```

The __init__() function sets the default option values and
initializes the parameter groups based on the input parameters.
Notice that we don't have to write any code to do this since
super(SGD, self).init(params, defaults) invokes the
base class initialization method. All we really need to do is
write the step() method. For each parameter group, we update
the parameters by first multiplying the parameters by the
group's LR and then subtracting the product from the
parameter itself. This is accomplished by calling p.add_(d_p,
alpha=-group['lr']).

Here's an example of how we would use our new optimizer:

```
optimizer = SimpleSGD(model.parameters(),
                      lr=0.001)
```

We could also define a different LR for different layers in the
model using the following code. Here we assume we're using
AlexNet again as the model with layers called feature and
classifier:

```
optimizer = SimpleSGD([
                {'params':
```

```
                    model.features.parameters()},
                {'params':
                 model.classifier.parameters(),
                 'lr': 1e-3}
            ], lr=1e-2)
```

Now that you can create your own optimizers for training your models, let's see how you can create your own custom training, validation, and test loops.

Custom Training, Validation, and Test Loops

All through this book, we've been using custom training, validation, and test loops. That's because in PyTorch all training, validation, and test loops are manually created by the programmer.

Unlike in Keras, there's no fit() or eval() method that exercises a loop. Instead, PyTorch requires that you write your own loops. This is actually a benefit in many cases because you'd like to control what happens during training.

In fact, the reference design in "Generative Learning—Generating Fashion-MNIST Images with DCGAN" on page 123 demonstrates how you can create a more complex training loop.

In this section, we'll explore a conventional way of writing loops and discuss common ways that developers customize their loops. Let's review some code commonly used for training, validation, and testing loops:

```
for epoch in range(n_epochs):

    # Training
    for data in train_dataloader:
        input, targets = data
        optimizer.zero_grad()
        output = model(input)
        train_loss = criterion(output, targets)
        train_loss.backward()
        optimizer.step()

    # Validation
    with torch.no_grad():
      for input, targets in val_dataloader:
```

```
            output = model(input)
            val_loss = criterion(output, targets)

  # Testing
  with torch.no_grad():
    for input, targets in test_dataloader:
        output = model(input)
        test_loss = criterion(output, targets)
```

This code should look familiar since we've used it often throughout the book. We assume that n_epochs, model, criterion, optimizer, and train_, val_, and test_dataloader have already been defined. For each epoch, we perform the training and validation loops. The training loop processes each batch one at a time, sends the batch input through the model, and computes the loss. We then perform backpropagation to compute the gradients and execute the optimizer to update the model's parameters.

The validation loop disables the gradient computation and passes the validation data through the network one batch at a time. The test loop passes the test data through the model one batch at a time and computes the loss for the test data.

Let's add some additional capabilities to our loops. The possibilities are endless, but this example will demonstrate some simple tasks like printing information, reconfiguring a model, and adjusting a hyperparameter in the middle of training. Let's walk through the following code to see how this is done:

```
for epoch in range(n_epochs):
    total_train_loss = 0.0  ❶
    total_val_loss = 0.0    ❶

    if (epoch == epoch//2):
      optimizer = optim.SGD(model.parameters(),
                            lr=0.001)  ❷
    # Training
    model.train()  ❸
    for data in train_dataloader:
        input, targets = data
        optimizer.zero_grad()
        output = model(input)
        train_loss = criterion(output, targets)
```

```
        train_loss.backward()
        optimizer.step()
        total_train_loss += train_loss ❶

    # Validation
    model.eval() ❸
    with torch.no_grad():
      for input, targets in val_dataloader:
          output = model(input)
          val_loss = criterion(output, targets)
          total_val_loss += val_loss ❶

    print("""Epoch: {}
        Train Loss: {}
        Val Loss {}""".format(
        epoch, total_train_loss,
        total_val_loss)) ❶

# Testing
model.eval()
with torch.no_grad():
  for input, targets in test_dataloader:
      output = model(input)
      test_loss = criterion(output, targets)
```

❶ Examples of printing epoch, training, and validation loss

❷ Examples of reconfiguring a model (best practice)

❸ Example of modifying a hyperparameter during training

In the preceding code, we added some variables to keep track of the running training and validation loss and we printed them for every epoch. Next we use the train() or eval() method to configure the model for training or evaluation, respectively. This only applies if the model's forward() function behaves differently for training and evaluation.

For example, some models may use dropout during training, but dropout should not be applied during validation or testing. In this case, we can reconfigure the model by calling model.train() or model.eval() before its execution.

Lastly, we modified the LR in our optimizer halfway through training. This enables us to train at a faster rate at first while fine-tuning our parameter updates after training on half of the epochs.

This example is a simple demonstration of how to customize your loops. Training, validation, and testing loops can be more complex as you train multiple networks simultaneously, use multimodal data, or design more complex networks that can even train other networks. PyTorch offers the flexibility to design special and innovative processes for training, validation, and testing.

TIP

PyTorch Lightning is a third-party PyTorch package that provides boilerplate templates for training, validation, and testing loops. The package provides a framework that allows you to create customized loops without having to repeatedly type the boilerplate code for each model implementation. We'll discuss PyTorch Lightning in Chapter 8. You can also find more information at the PyTorch Lightning website (*http://pytorch.tips/pytorch-lightning*).

In this chapter, you learned how to create your own custom components for developing deep learning models in PyTorch. As your models grow more and more complex, you may find that the time you need to train your model may become quite long—perhaps days or even weeks. In the next chapter, you'll see how to use built-in PyTorch capabilities to accelerate and optimize your training process to significantly reduce your overall model development time.

## CHAPTER 6

PyTorch Acceleration and Optimization

In the previous chapters, you learned how to use the built-in capabilities of PyTorch and extend those capabilities by creating your own custom components for deep learning. Doing so enables you to quickly design new models and algorithms to train them.

However, when dealing with very large datasets or more complex models, training your models on a single CPU or GPU can take an extremely long time—it may take days or even weeks to get preliminary results. Longer training times can become frustrating, especially when you want to conduct many experiments using different hyperparameter configurations.

In this chapter, we'll explore state-of-the-art techniques to accelerate and optimize your model development with PyTorch. First, we'll look at using tensor processing units (TPUs) instead of GPU devices and consider instances in which using TPUs can improve performance. Next, I'll show you how to use PyTorch's built-in capabilities for parallel processing and distributed training. This will provide a quick reference for training models across multiple GPUs and multiple machines so you can quickly scale your training when more hardware resources are available. After exploring ways to accelerate training, we'll look at how to optimize your models using advanced techniques like hyperparameter tuning, quantization, and pruning.

The chapter will also provide reference code to make getting started easy, and references to the key packages and libraries we've used. Once you create your models and training loops, you can return to this chapter for tips on how to accelerate and optimize your training process.

Let's begin by exploring how to run your models on TPUs.

PyTorch on a TPU

As deep learning and AI are increasingly deployed, companies are developing custom hardware chips or ASICs aimed at optimizing model performance in hardware. Google developed its own ASIC for NN acceleration called the TPU. Since the TPU was designed for NNs, it does not have some of the downfalls of the GPU, which was designed for graphics processing. Google's TPU is now available for you to use as part of Google Cloud TPU. You can also run Google Colab with a TPU.

In the previous chapters, I showed you how to test and train your deep models using a GPU. You should continue to use CPUs and GPUs for training if the following conditions apply to your use case:

- You have small- or medium-size models with small batch sizes.

- Your models do not take long to train.

- Moving data in and out is your main bottleneck.

- Your calculations are frequently branching or mostly done element-wise, or you use sparse memory access.

- You need to use high precision. Doubles are not suitable for TPUs.

On the other hand, there are several reasons why you may want to use a TPU instead of a GPU for training. TPUs are very fast at performing dense vector and matrix computations. They are optimized for specific workloads. You should strongly consider using TPUs when the following apply to your use case:

- Your model is dominated by matrix computations.

- Your model has long training times.

- You want to run multiple iterations of your entire training loop on TPUs.

Running on a TPU is very similar to running on a CPU or a GPU. Let's revisit how we would train the model on a GPU in the following code:

```
device = torch.device("cuda" if
  torch.cuda.is_available() else "cpu")  ❶

model.to(device)  ❷
for epoch in range(n_epochs):
  for data in trainloader:
    input, labels = data
    input = input.to(device)  ❸
    labels = labels.to(device)  ❸
    optimizer.zero_grad()

    output = model(input)

    loss = criterion(input, labels)
    loss.backward()
    optimizer.step()
```

❶ Configure the device to a GPU if it's available.

❷ Send the model to the device.

❸ Send inputs and labels to the GPU.

Namely, we move the model, inputs, and labels to the GPU, and the rest is done for us. Training your network on a TPU is almost the same as training it on a GPU except you will need to use the *PyTorch/XLA* (Accelerated Linear Algebra) package as TPUs are not currently supported natively by PyTorch.

Let's train our model on a Cloud TPU using Google Colab. Open a new Colab notebook and select Change Runtime Type from the Runtime menu. Then select TPU from the "Hardware accelerator" drop-down menu, as shown in Figure 6-1. Google Colab provides a free Cloud TPU system, including a remote CPU host and four TPU chips with two cores each.

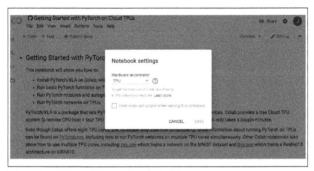

Figure 6-1. Using a TPU in Google Colab

Since Colab does not have PyTorch/XLA installed by default we'll need to install that first, using the following commands. This installs the latest "nightly" version, but you can select another version if needed:

```
&#33;curl 'https://raw.githubusercontent.com/pytorch' \
  '/xla/master/contrib/scripts/env-setup.py' \
  -o pytorch-xla-env-setup.py
&#33;python pytorch-xla-env-setup.py --version &#34;nightly&#34;  ❶
```

<1>These are commands that are intended to run in a notebook. Omit the "!" to run them on the command line.

Once PyTorch/XLA is installed, we can import the package and move our data to the TPU:

```
import torch_xla.core.xla_model as xm

device = xm.xla_device()
```

Notice that we do not use `torch.cuda.is_available()` here, since it only works for GPUs. Unfortunately, there is no `is_available()` method for TPUs. If your environment is not configured for TPUs, you will get an error.

Once the device is set, the rest of the code is exactly the same:

```
model.to(device)
for epoch in range(n_epochs):
  for data in trainloader:
    input, labels = data
    input = input.to(device)
    labels = labels.to(device)
    optimizer.zero_grad()

    output = model(input)

    loss = criterion(input, labels)
    loss.backward()
    optimizer.step()

print(output.device)  ❶
# out: xla:1
```

❶ If Colab is configured for TPUs, you should see xla:1.

PyTorch/XLA is a general library for XLA operations and may support other specialized ASICs in addition to TPUs. For more information on PyTorch/XLA, visit the PyTorch/XLA GitHub repository (*https://pytorch.tips/xla*).

There are still many limitations for running on TPUs, and GPU support is more widespread. Therefore, most PyTorch developers will benchmark their code using a single GPU at first and then explore using a single TPU or multiple GPUs to accelerate their code.

We've already covered using a single GPU earlier in this book. In the next section, I'll show you how to train your models on machines with multiple GPUs.

PyTorch on Multiple GPUs (Single Machine)

When accelerating your training and development, it's important to make the most of the hardware resources you have available. If you have a local machine or a network server with access to multiple GPUs, this section will show you how to fully utilize the GPUs on your system. In addition, you may want to scale your GPU resources by using cloud GPUs on a single instance. This is usually the first level of scaling before considering a distributed training approach.

Running your code across multiple GPUs is often called *parallel processing*. There are two approaches to parallel processing: *data* parallel processing and *model* parallel processing. During data parallel processing, the data batches are split between multiple GPUs while each GPU runs a copy of the model. During model parallel processing, the model is split up between multiple GPUs and the data batches are pipelined into each portion.

Data parallel processing is more commonly used in practice. Model parallel processing is often reserved for cases in which the model does not fit on a single GPU. I'll show you how to perform both types of processing in this section.

Data Parallel Processing

Figure 6-2 illustrates how data parallel processing works. In this process, each data batch is split into N parts (N is the number of GPUs available on the host). N is typically a power of two. Each GPU holds a copy of the model, and the gradients and loss are computed for each portion of the batch. The gradients and loss are combined at the end of each iteration. This approach is good for larger batch sizes and use cases in which the model will fit on a single GPU.

Data parallel processing can be implemented in PyTorch using a *single-process, multithreaded approach* or by using a *multiprocess* approach. The single-process, multithreaded approach requires only one additional line of code but does not perform well in many cases.

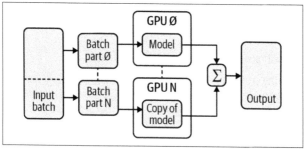

Figure 6-2. Data parallel processing

Unfortunately, multithreading performs poorly due to Python's Global Interpreter Lock (GIL) contention across threads, the per-iteration replication of the model, and the additional overhead introduced by scattering inputs and gathering outputs. You may want to try this approach because it's so simple, but in most cases, you will probably use the multiprocess approach.

The multithreaded approach using nn.DataParallel

The multithreaded approach to data parallel processing is natively supported by PyTorch's nn module. All you need to do is wrap your model in nn.DataParallel before sending it to the GPU, as shown in the following code. Here we assume you have already instantiated your model:

```
if torch.cuda.device_count() > 1:
  print("This machine has",
        torch.cuda.device_count(),
        "GPUs available.")
  model = nn.DataParallel(model)

model.to("cuda")
```

First we check to make sure we have multiple GPUs, and then we use nn.DataParallel() to set up data parallel processing before sending the model to the GPU with to(*device*).

This multithreaded approach is the simplest way to run on multiple GPUs; however, the multiprocess approach usually performs better, even on a single machine. In addition, the multiprocess approach can also be used to run across multiple machines, as we'll see later in this chapter.

The multiprocess approach using DDP (preferred)

Training your models across multiple GPUs is best accomplished using a multiprocess approach. PyTorch supports this with its nn.parallel.DistributedDataProcessing module. Distributed data processing (DDP) can be used with multiple processes on a single machine or with multiple processes across multiple machines. We'll start with a single machine.

There are four steps you need to do to modify your code:

1. Initialize a process group using *torch.distributed*.

2. Create a local model using *torch.nn.to()*.

3. Wrap the model with DDP using *torch.nn.parallel*.

4. Spawn processes using *torch.multiprocessing*.

The following code demonstrates how you can convert your model for DDP training. We'll break it down into steps. First, import the necessary libraries:

```
import torch
import torch.distributed as dist
import torch.multiprocessing as mp
import torch.nn as nn
import torch.optim as optim
from torch.nn.parallel \
    import DistributedDataParallel as DDP
```

Notice that we're using three new libraries—*torch.distributed*, *torch.multiprocessing*, and *torch.nn.parallel*. The following code shows you how to create a distributed training loop:

```
def dist_training_loop(rank,
                       world_size,
                       dataloader,
                       model,
```

```
                        loss_fn,
                        optimizer):
    dist.init_process_group("gloo",
                        rank=rank,
                        world_size=world_size) ❶

    model = model.to(rank) ❷
    ddp_model = DDP(model,
                        device_ids=[rank]) ❸
    optimizer = optimizer(
                        ddp_model.parameters(),
                        lr=0.001)

    for epochs in range(n_epochs):
        for input, labels in dataloader:
            input = input.to(rank)
            labels = labels.to(rank) ❹
            optimizer.zero_grad()
            outputs = ddp_model(input) ❺
            loss = loss_fn(outputs, labels)
            loss.backward()
            optimizer.step()

    dist.destroy_process_group()
```

❶ Set up a process group with world_size processes.

❷ Move the model to a GPU with the ID of rank.

❸ Wrap the model in DDP.

❹ Move inputs and labels to the GPU with the ID of rank.

❺ Call the DDP model for the forward pass.

DDP broadcasts the model states from the rank0 process to all the other processes, so we don't have to worry about the different processes having models with different initialized weights.

DDP handles the lower-level interprocess communications that allow you to treat the model as if it was a local model. During the backward pass, DDP automatically synchronizes the gradients and places the synchronized gradient tensor in params.grad when loss.backward() returns.

Now that we have the process defined, we need to create these processes using the spawn() function, as shown in the following code:

```
if __name__=="__main__":
  world_size = 2
  mp.spawn(dist_training_loop,
      args=(world_size,),
      nprocs=world_size,
      join=True)
```

Here, we run the code as main to spawn two processes, each with its own GPU. And that's how you run data parallel processing on multiple GPUs on a single machine.

WARNING

GPU devices cannot be shared across processes.

If your model does not fit into a single GPU or you are using smaller batch sizes, you may consider using model parallel processing instead of data parallel processing. We'll look at that next.

Model Parallel Processing

Figure 6-3 illustrates how model parallel processing works. In this process, the model is split across N GPUs on the same machine. If we process data batches in sequence, the next GPU will always be waiting for the previous GPU to finish, and this defeats the purpose of parallel processing. Therefore, we need to pipeline the data processing so that every GPU is running at any given moment. When we pipeline the data, only the first N batches are run in sequence, and then each subsequent run activates all the GPUs.

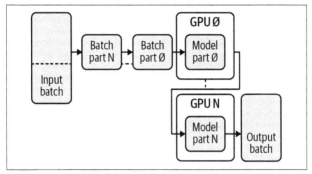

Figure 6-3. Model parallel processing

Implementing model parallel processing is not as simple as data parallel processing, and it requires you to rewrite your models. You'll need to define how your models are split across multiple GPUs and how the data will be pipelined in the forward pass. This is typically done by writing a subclass for your model with a multi-GPU implementation for a specific number of GPUs.

The following code demonstrates a two-GPU implementation of AlexNet:

```
class TwoGPUAlexNet(AlexNet):
    def __init__(self):
        super(ModelParallelAlexNet, self).__init__(
                num_classes=num_classes,
                *args,
                **kwargs)
        self.features.to('cuda:0')
        self.avgpool.to('cuda:0')
        self.classifier.to('cuda:1')
        self.split_size = split_size

    def forward(self, x):
        splits = iter(x.split(self.split_size,
                        dim=0))
        s_next = next(splits)
        s_prev = self.seq1(s_next).to('cuda:1')
        ret = []

        for s_next in splits:
```

```
            s_prev = self.seq2(s_prev)  ❶
            ret.append(self.fc(
                s_prev.view(s_prev.size(0), -1)))

            s_prev = self.seq1(s_next).to('cuda:1')  ❷

        s_prev = self.seq2(s_prev)
        ret.append(self.fc(
            s_prev.view(s_prev.size(0), -1)))

        return torch.cat(ret)
```

❶ s_prev runs on cuda:1.

❷ s_next runs on cuda:0, which can run concurrently with s_prev.

Because we are deriving a subclass from the AlexNet class, we inherit its model structure, so there's no need to create our layers. Instead, we need to describe which pieces of the model go on GPU0 and which pieces go on GPU1 in the __init__() constructor. Then we need to pipeline the data through each GPU in the forward() method to implement GPU pipelining. When you train your model, you will need to put labels on the last GPU, as shown in the following code:

```
model = TwoGPUAlexNet()
loss_fn = nn.MSELoss()
optimizer = optim.SGD(model.parameters(), lr=0.001)

for epochs in range(n_epochs):
  for input, labels in dataloader;
    input = input.to("cuda:0")
    labels = labels.to("cuda:1")  ❶
    optimizer.zero_grad()
    outputs = model(input)
    loss_fn(outputs, labels).backward()
    optimizer.step()
```

❶ Send inputs to GPU0 and labels to GPU1.

As you can see, the training loop requires changing one line of code to make sure the labels are on the last GPU since that's where the outputs will be before calculating the loss.

Data parallel processing and model parallel processing are two effective paradigms for leveraging multiple GPUs for accelerated training. Wouldn't it be great if we could combine the two approaches and achieve even better results? Let's see how to implement the combined approach.

Combined Data Parallel Processing and Model Parallel Processing

You can combine data parallel processing with model parallel processing to further improve performance. In this case, you will wrap your model using DDP to distribute your data batches among multiple processes. Each process will use multiple GPUs, and your model will be partitioned among each of those GPUs.

There are only two changes we need to make:

1. Change our multi-GPU model class to accept devices as inputs.

2. Omit setting the output device during the forward pass. DDP will determine where the input and output data will be placed.

The following code shows how to modify the multi-GPU model:

```python
class Simple2GPUModel(nn.Module):
    def __init__(self, dev0, dev1):
        super(Simple2GPUModel,
            self).__init__()
        self.dev0 = dev0
        self.dev1 = dev1
        self.net1 = torch.nn.Linear(
                    10, 10).to(dev0)
        self.relu = torch.nn.ReLU()
        self.net2 = torch.nn.Linear(
                    10, 5).to(dev1)

    def forward(self, x):
        x = x.to(self.dev0)
        x = self.relu(self.net1(x))
```

```
            x = x.to(self.dev1)
            return self.net2(x)
```

In the __init__() constructor we pass in the GPU device objects, dev0 and dev1, and describe which parts of the model reside in which GPUs. This allows us to instantiate new models on different processes, each with two GPUs. The forward() method moves the data from one GPU to the next at the proper point in the model.

The training loop changes are shown in the following code:

```
def model_parallel_training(rank, world_size):
    print(f"Running DDP with a model parallel")
    setup(rank, world_size)

    # set up mp_model and devices for this process
    dev0 = rank * 2
    dev1 = rank * 2 + 1
    mp_model = Simple2GPUModel(dev0, dev1)
    ddp_mp_model = DDP(mp_model)  ❶

    loss_fn = nn.MSELoss()
    optimizer = optim.SGD(
            ddp_mp_model.parameters(), lr=0.001)

    for epochs in range(n_epochs):
      for input, labels in dataloader:
        input = input.to(dev0),
        labels = labels,to(dev1)  ❷
        optimizer.zero_grad()
        outputs = ddp_mp_model(input)  ❸
        loss = loss_fn(outputs, labels)
        loss.backward()
        optimizer.step()

    cleanup()
```

❶ Wrap the model in DDP.

❷ Move the inputs and labels to the appropriate device IDs.

❸ The output is on dev1.

To recap, you have a few options when using PyTorch across multiple GPUs. You can use the reference code in this section

---

to implement data parallel, model parallel, or combined parallel processing to accelerate your model training and inference. So far, we've only discussed multiple GPUs on a single machine or a cloud instance.

In many cases, parallel processing across multiple GPUs on a single machine can reduce training times by half or more—all you need to do is upgrade your GPU card or utilize a larger cloud GPU instance. However, if you are training very complex models or using extremely large datasets, you may want to use multiple machines or cloud instances to speed up your training.

The good news is that DDP on multiple machines is not much different than DDP on a single machine. The next section shows how this is done.

Distributed Training (Multiple Machines)

If training your NN models on a single machine does not meet your needs and you have access to a cluster of servers, you can use PyTorch's distributed processing capabilities to scale your training across multiple machines. PyTorch's distributed subpackage, `torch.distributed`, provides a rich set of capabilities to suit a variety of training architectures and hardware platforms.

The `torch.distributed` subpackage consists of three components: DDP, RPC-based distributed training (RPC), and collective communication (c10d). We used DDP in the previous section to run multiple processes on a single machine, and it's best suited for the data parallel processing paradigm. RPC was created to support more general training architectures and can be used for distributed architectures other than the data parallel processing paradigm.

The c10d component is a communications library used to transfer tensors across processes. c10d is used by both the DDP and RPC components as a backend, and PyTorch provides a c10d API so you can use it in custom distributed applications.

In this book, we'll focus on using DDP for distributed training. However, if you have a more advanced use case, you may want to use RPC or c10d. You can find out more about these by reading the PyTorch documentation (*https://pytorch.tips/rpc*).

For distributed training with DDP, we will follow the same DDP procedure as we did for a single machine with multiple processes. However, in this case, we will run each process on a separate machine or instance.

To run across multiple machines, we run DDP with a launch script that specifies our configuration. The launch script is contained in `torch.distributed` and can be executed as shown in the following code. Let's assume you have two nodes, Node 0 and Node 1. Node 0 is the master node and has an IP address of 192.168.1.1 and a free port at 1234. On Node 0, you would run the following script:

```
>>> python -m torch.distributed.launch
        --nproc_per_node=NUM_GPUS
        --nnodes=2
        --node_rank=0  ❶
        --master_addr="192.168.1.1"
        --master_port=1234
        TRAINING_SCRIPT.py (--arg1 --arg2 --arg3)
```

❶ node_rank is set to Node 0.

On Node 1, you would run this next script. Notice that this node's rank is 1:

```
>>> python -m torch.distributed.launch
        --nproc_per_node=NUM_GPUS
        --nnodes=2
        --node_rank=1  ❶
        --master_addr="192.168.1.1"
        --master_port=1234
        TRAINING_SCRIPT.py (--arg1 --arg2 --arg3)
```

❶ node_rank is set to Node 1.

If you'd like to explore the optional parameters in this script, run the following command:

```
>>> python -m torch.distributed.launch --help
```

Remember, if you are not using a DDP paradigm, you should consider using the RPC or c10d API for your use case. Parallel processing and distributed training can significantly speed up model performance and reduce development time. In the next section, we'll consider other ways to improve NN performance by implementing techniques that optimize the model itself.

Model Optimization

Model optimization is an advanced topic that focuses on the underlying implementation of NN models and how they are trained. As research in this space continues to evolve, PyTorch has added various capabilities for model optimization. In this section, we'll explore three areas of optimization—hyperparameter tuning, quantization, and pruning—and provide reference code for you to use in your own designs.

Hyperparameter Tuning

Deep learning model development often involves selecting many variables that are used to design a model and how it's trained. These variables are called *hyperparameters* and can include architecture variations like the number of layers, layer depth, and kernel sizes, as well as optional stages like pooling or batch normalization. Hyperparameters may also include variations of loss functions or optimization parameters, such as LRs or weight decay rates.

In this section, I'll show you how to use a package called Ray Tune to manage your hyperparameter optimization. Researchers often test a small set of hyperparameters manually. However, Ray Tune allows you to configure your hyperparameters and determines which settings are best for performance.

Ray Tune supports state-of-the-art hyperparameter search algorithms and distributed training. It is constantly being updated with new capabilities. Let's see how we can use Ray Tune to perform hyperparameter tuning.

Remember the LeNet5 model we trained for image classification back in Chapter 3? Let's experiment with different model configurations and training parameters to see if we can use hyperparameter tuning to improve our model.

In order to use Ray Tune, we need to make the following changes to our model:

1. Define our hyperparameters and their search space.

2. Write a function to wrap our training loop.

3. Run Ray Tune hyperparameter tuning.

Let's redefine our model so that we can configure the number of nodes in the fully connected layers, as shown in the following code:

```python
import torch.nn as nn
import torch.nn.functional as F

class Net(nn.Module):
    def __init__(self, nodes_1=120, nodes_2=84):
        super(Net, self).__init__()
        self.conv1 = nn.Conv2d(3, 6, 5)
        self.pool = nn.MaxPool2d(2, 2)
        self.conv2 = nn.Conv2d(6, 16, 5)
        self.fc1 = nn.Linear(16 * 5 * 5, nodes_1)  ❶
        self.fc2 = nn.Linear(nodes_1, nodes_2)  ❷
        self.fc3 = nn.Linear(nodes_2, 10)

    def forward(self, x):
        x = self.pool(F.relu(self.conv1(x)))
        x = self.pool(F.relu(self.conv2(x)))
        x = x.view(-1, 16 * 5 * 5)
        x = F.relu(self.fc1(x))
        x = F.relu(self.fc2(x))
        x = self.fc3(x)
        return x
```

❶ Configure nodes in `fc1`.

❷ Configure nodes in `fc2`.

So far we have two hyperparameters, nodes_1 and nodes_2. Let's also define two more hyperparameters, `lr` and `batch_size`, so we can vary the learning rate and batch size used in our training.

In the following code, we import the `ray` package and define the hyperparameter configuration:

```
from ray import tune
import numpy as np

config = {
  "nodes_1": tune.sample_from(
      lambda _: 2 ** np.random.randint(2, 9)),
  "nodes_2": tune.sample_from(
      lambda _: 2 ** np.random.randint(2, 9)),
  "lr": tune.loguniform(1e-4, 1e-1),
  "batch_size": tune.choice([2, 4, 8, 16])
  }
```

During each run, the values for these parameters are chosen from the specified search space. You can use the method `tune.sample_from()` and a lambda function to define a search space, or you can use built-in sampling functions. In this case, `layer_1` and `layer_2` are each set to a random value from 2 to 9 using `sample_from()`.

The `lr` and `batch_size` use built-in functions in which `lr` is randomly chosen to be a double from 1e-4 to 1e-1 with uniform distribution, and `batch_size` is randomly chosen to be either 2, 4, 8, or 16.

Next we need to wrap our training loop with a function that takes the configuration dictionary as an input. This training loop function will be called by Ray Tune.

Before we write our training loop, let's define a function that loads the CIFAR-10 data so we can reuse the data from the same directory during training. The following code is similar to the data-loading code we used in Chapter 3:

```python
import torch
import torchvision
from torchvision import transforms

def load_data(data_dir="./data"):
    train_transforms = transforms.Compose([
        transforms.RandomCrop(32, padding=4),
        transforms.RandomHorizontalFlip(),
        transforms.ToTensor(),
        transforms.Normalize(
            (0.4914, 0.4822, 0.4465),
            (0.2023, 0.1994, 0.2010))])

    test_transforms = transforms.Compose([
        transforms.ToTensor(),
        transforms.Normalize(
            (0.4914, 0.4822, 0.4465),
            (0.2023, 0.1994, 0.2010))])

    trainset = torchvision.datasets.CIFAR10(
        root=data_dir, train=True,
        download=True, transform=train_transforms)

    testset = torchvision.datasets.CIFAR10(
        root=data_dir, train=False,
        download=True, transform=test_transforms)

    return trainset, testset
```

Now we can wrap our training loop into a function, *train_model()*, as shown in the following code. This is a large snippet of code; however, it should be familiar to you:

```python
from torch import optim
from torch import nn
from torch.utils.data import random_split

def train_model(config):
    device = torch.device("cuda" if
        torch.cuda.is_available() else "cpu")

    model = Net(config['nodes_1'],
        config['nodes_2']).to(device=device)  ❶

    criterion = nn.CrossEntropyLoss()
    optimizer = optim.SGD(model.parameters(),
```

```
                         lr=config['lr'],
                         momentum=0.9) ❷

trainset, testset = load_data()

test_abs = int(len(trainset) * 0.8)
train_subset, val_subset = random_split(
    trainset,
    [test_abs, len(trainset) - test_abs])

trainloader = torch.utils.data.DataLoader(
    train_subset,
    batch_size=int(config["batch_size"]),
    shuffle=True) ❸

valloader = torch.utils.data.DataLoader(
    val_subset,
    batch_size=int(config["batch_size"]),
    shuffle=True) ❸

for epoch in range(10):
    train_loss = 0.0
    epoch_steps = 0
    for data in trainloader:
        inputs, labels = data
        inputs = inputs.to(device)
        labels = labels.to(device)

        optimizer.zero_grad()

        outputs = model(inputs)
        loss = criterion(outputs, labels)
        loss.backward()
        optimizer.step()
        train_loss += loss.item()

    val_loss = 0.0
    total = 0
    correct = 0
    for data in valloader:
        with torch.no_grad():
            inputs, labels = data
            inputs = inputs.to(device)
            labels = labels.to(device)

            outputs = model(inputs)
            _, predicted = torch.max(
                        outputs.data, 1)
            total += labels.size(0)
```

```
              correct += \
                (predicted == labels).sum().item()

              loss = criterion(outputs, labels)
              val_loss += loss.cpu().numpy()

      print(f'epoch: {epoch} ',
            f'train_loss: ',
            f'{train_loss/len(trainloader)}',
            f'val_loss: ',
            f'{val_loss/len(valloader)}',
            f'val_acc: {correct/total}')
      tune.report(loss=(val_loss / len(valloader)),
                  accuracy=correct / total)
```

❶ Make the model layers configurable.

❷ Make the learning rate configurable.

❸ Make the batch size configurable.

Next we want to run Ray Tune, but we first need to determine the scheduler and the reporter that we want to use. The scheduler determines how Ray Tune searches and selects the hyperparameters, while the reporter specifies how we'd like to view the results. Let's set them up in the following code:

```
from ray.tune import CLIReporter
from ray.tune.schedulers import ASHAScheduler

scheduler = ASHAScheduler(
    metric="loss",
    mode="min",
    max_t=10,
    grace_period=1,
    reduction_factor=2)

reporter = CLIReporter(
    metric_columns=["loss",
                    "accuracy",
                    "training_iteration"])
```

For the scheduler, we'll use the asynchronous successive halving algorithm (ASHA) for hyperparameter searches and instruct it to minimize loss. For the reporter, we'll configure a

---

CLI reporter to report the loss, accuracy, training iteration, and selected hyperparameters on the CLI for each run.

Finally we can run Ray Tune using the `run()` method as shown in the following code:

```
from functools import partial

result = tune.run(
    partial(train_model),
    resources_per_trial={"cpu": 2, "gpu": 1},
    config=config,
    num_samples=10,
    scheduler=scheduler,
    progress_reporter=reporter)
```

We provision the resources and specify the configuration. We pass in our configuration dictionary, specify the number of samples or runs, and pass in our `scheduler` and `reporter` functions.

Ray Tune will report the results. The `get_best_trial()` method returns an object that contains information about the best trial. We can print out the hyperparameter settings that yielded the best results, as shown in the following code:

```
best_trial = result.get_best_trial(
    "loss", "min", "last")
print("Best trial config: {}".format(
    best_trial.config))
print("Best trial final validation loss:",
      "{}".format(
          best_trial.last_result["loss"]))
print("Best trial final validation accuracy:",
      "{}".format(
          best_trial.last_result["accuracy"]))
```

You may find other features of the Ray Tune API useful. Table 6-1 lists the available schedulers in `tune.schedulers`.

Table 6-1. Ray Tune schedulers

Scheduling method	Description
ASHA	Scheduler that runs the asynchronous successive halving algorithm
HyperBand	Scheduler that runs the HyperBand early stopping algorithm
Median Stopping Rule	Scheduler based on the median stopping rule, as described in "Google Vizier: A Service for Black-Box Optimization" (*https://research.google.com/pubs/pub46180.html*).
Population Based Training	Scheduler based on the Population Based Training algorithm
Population Based Training Replay	Scheduler that replays a Population Based Training run
BOHB	Scheduler that uses Bayesian optimization and HyperBand
FIFOScheduler	Simple scheduler that just runs trials in submission order
TrialScheduler	Scheduler based on trials
Shim Instantiation	Scheduler based on the provided string

More information can be found in the Ray Tune documentation. (*https://pytorch.tips/ray*) As you can see, Ray Tune has a rich set of capabilities, but there are other hyperparameter packages that support PyTorch as well. These include Allegro Trains (*https://pytorch.tips/allegro*) and Optuna (*https://pytorch.tips/optuna*).

Hyperparameter tuning can significantly improve the performance of an NN model by finding the settings that work best. Next, we'll explore another technique to optimize a model: quantization.

Quantization

NNs are implemented as computational graphs, and their computations often use 32-bit (or in some cases, 64-bit) floating-point numbers. However, we can enable our computations to use lower-precision numbers and still achieve comparable results by applying quantization.

Quantization refers to techniques for computing and accessing memory with lower-precision data. These techniques can decrease model size, reduce memory bandwidth, and perform faster inference due to savings in memory bandwidth and faster computing with int8 arithmetic.

A quick quantization method is to reduce all computation precision by half. Let's consider our LeNet5 model example again, as shown in the following code:

```python
import torch
from torch import nn
import torch.nn.functional as F

class LeNet5(nn.Module):
    def __init__(self):
        super(LeNet5, self).__init__()
        self.conv1 = nn.Conv2d(3, 6, 5)
        self.conv2 = nn.Conv2d(6, 16, 5)
        self.fc1 = nn.Linear(16 * 5 * 5, 120)
        self.fc2 = nn.Linear(120, 84)
        self.fc3 = nn.Linear(84, 10)

    def forward(self, x):
        x = F.max_pool2d(
            F.relu(self.conv1(x)), (2, 2))
        x = F.max_pool2d(
            F.relu(self.conv2(x)), 2)
        x = x.view(-1,
                    int(x.nelement() / x.shape[0]))
        x = F.relu(self.fc1(x))
        x = F.relu(self.fc2(x))
        x = self.fc3(x)
        return x

model = LeNet5()
```

By default, all computations and memory are implemented as float32. We can inspect the data types of our model's parameters using the following code:

```
for n, p in model.named_parameters():
  print(n, ": ", p.dtype)

# out:
# conv1.weight :  torch.float32
# conv1.bias :  torch.float32
# conv2.weight :  torch.float32
# conv2.bias :  torch.float32
# fc1.weight :  torch.float32
# fc1.bias :  torch.float32
# fc2.weight :  torch.float32
# fc2.bias :  torch.float32
# fc3.weight :  torch.float32
# fc3.bias :  torch.float32
```

As expected, our data types are float32. However, we can reduce the model to half precision in one line of code using the half() method:

```
model = model.half()

for n, p in model.named_parameters():
  print(n, ": ", p.dtype)

# out:
# conv1.weight :  torch.float16
# conv1.bias :  torch.float16
# conv2.weight :  torch.float16
# conv2.bias :  torch.float16
# fc1.weight :  torch.float16
# fc1.bias :  torch.float16
# fc2.weight :  torch.float16
# fc2.bias :  torch.float16
# fc3.weight :  torch.float16
# fc3.bias :  torch.float16
```

Now our computation and memory values are float16 . Using half() is often a quick and easy way to quantize your models. It's worth a try to see if the performance is adequate for your use case.

However, in many cases, we don't want to quantize every computation in the same way, and we may need to quantize beyond float16 values. For these other cases, PyTorch provides three additional modes of quantization: dynamic quantization, post-training static quantization, and quantization-aware training (QAT).

Dynamic quantization is used when throughput is limited by compute or memory bandwidth for weights. This is often true for LSTM, RNN, Bidirectional Encoder Representations from Transformers (BERT), or Transformer networks. Static quantization is used when throughput is limited by memory bandwidth for activations and often applies for CNNs. QAT is used when accuracy requirements cannot be achieved by static quantization.

Let's provide some reference code for each type. All types convert weights to int8. They vary in handle activations and memory access.

Dynamic quantization is the easiest type. It converts the activations to int8 on the fly. Computations use efficient int8 values, but the activations are read and written to memory in floating-point format.

The following code shows you how to quantize a model with dynamic quantization:

```
import torch.quantization

quantized_model = \
  torch.quantization.quantize_dynamic(
      model,
      {torch.nn.Linear},
      dtype=torch.qint8)
```

All we need to do is pass in our model and specify the quantized layers and the quantization level.

Post-training static quantization can be used to further reduce latency by observing the distributions of different activations during training and by deciding how those activations should be quantized at the time of inference. This type of quantization allows us to pass quantized values between operations without converting back and forth between floats and ints in memory:

```
static_quant_model = LeNet5()
static_quant_model.qconfig = \
  torch.quantization.get_default_qconfig('fbgemm')

torch.quantization.prepare(
    static_quant_model, inplace=True)
torch.quantization.convert(
    static_quant_model, inplace=True)
```

Post-training static quantization requires configuration and training to prepare it before its use. We configure the backend to use x86 (fbgemm) and call `torch.quantization.prepare` to insert observers to calibrate the model and collect statistics. Then we convert the model to a quantized version.

Quantization-aware training typically results in the best accuracy. In this case, all weights and activations are "fake quantized" during the forward and backward pass of training. Float values are rounded to the int8 equivalent, but the computations are still done in floating point. That is, the weight adjustments are made "aware" that they will be quantized during training. The following code shows how to quantize a model with QAT:

```
qat_model = LeNet5()
qat_mode.qconfig = \
  torch.quantization.get_default_qat_qconfig('fbgemm')

torch.quantization.prepare_qat(
    qat_model, inplace=True)
torch.quantization.convert(
    qat_model, inplace=True)
```

Again we need to configure the backend and prepare the model, and then we call `convert()` to quantize the model.

PyTorch's quantization capabilities are continuing to evolve, and they currently exist in beta. Please refer to the PyTorch documentation (*https://pytorch.tips/quantization*) for the latest information on how to use the Quantization package.

Pruning

Modern deep learning models can have millions of parameters and can be difficult to deploy. However, models are over-parameterized, and parameters can often be reduced without affecting the accuracy or model performance much. *Pruning* is a technique that reduces the number of model parameters with minimal effect on performance. This allows you to deploy models with less memory, lower power usage, and reduced hardware resources.

Pruning model example

Pruning can be applied to an `nn.module`. Since an `nn.module` may consist of a single layer, multiple layers, or an entire model, pruning can be applied to a single layer, multiple layers, or the entire model itself. Let's consider our example LeNet5 model:

```
from torch import nn
import torch.nn.functional as F

class LeNet5(nn.Module):
    def __init__(self):
        super(LeNet5, self).__init__()
        self.conv1 = nn.Conv2d(3, 6, 5)
        self.conv2 = nn.Conv2d(6, 16, 5)
```

```
        self.fc1 = nn.Linear(16 * 5 * 5, 120)
        self.fc2 = nn.Linear(120, 84)
        self.fc3 = nn.Linear(84, 10)

    def forward(self, x):
        x = F.max_pool2d(
            F.relu(self.conv1(x)), (2, 2))
        x = F.max_pool2d(
            F.relu(self.conv2(x)), 2)
        x = x.view(-1,
                   int(x.nelement() / x.shape[0]))
        x = F.relu(self.fc1(x))
        x = F.relu(self.fc2(x))
        x = self.fc3(x)
        return x
```

Our LeNet5 model has five submodules—conv1, conv2, fc1, fc2, and fc3. The model parameters consist of its weights and biases and can be shown using the named_parameters() method. Let's look at the parameters of the conv1 layer:

```
device = torch.device("cuda" if
  torch.cuda.is_available() else "cpu")
model = LeNet5().to(device)

print(list(model.conv1.named_parameters()))
# out:
# [('weight', Parameter containing:
# tensor([[[[0.0560, 0.0066, ..., 0.0183, 0.0783]]]],
#         device='cuda:0',
#         requires_grad=True)),
#  ('bias', Parameter containing:
# tensor([0.0754, -0.0356, ..., -0.0111, 0.0984],
#         device='cuda:0',
#         requires_grad=True))]
```

Local and global pruning

Local pruning is when we only prune a specific piece of our model. With this technique we can apply local pruning to a single layer or module. Just call your pruning method, passing in the layer, and set its options as shown in the following code:

```
import torch.nn.utils.prune as prune

prune.random_unstructured(model.conv1,
                          name="weight",
                          amount=0.25)
```

This example applies random unstructured pruning to the parameters named `weight` in the `conv1` layer in our model. This only prunes the weight parameters. We can prune the bias parameters as well with the following code:

```
prune.random_unstructured(model.conv1,
                          name="bias",
                          amount=0.25)
```

Pruning can be applied iteratively, so you can further prune the same parameters using other pruning methods across different dimensions.

You can prune modules and parameters differently. For example, you may want to prune by module or layer type and apply pruning to convolutional layers differently than linear layers. The following code illustrates one way to do so:

```
model = LeNet5().to(device)

for name, module in model.named_modules():
    if isinstance(module, torch.nn.Conv2d):
        prune.random_unstructured(module,
                                  name='weight',
                                  amount=0.3) ❶
    elif isinstance(module, torch.nn.Linear):
        prune.random_unstructured(module,
                                  name='weight',
                                  amount=0.5) ❷
```

❶ Prune all 2D convolutional layers by 30%.

❷ Prune all linear layers by 50%.

Another use of the pruning API is to apply *global pruning*, in which we apply a pruning method to the entire model. For example, we could prune 25% of our model's parameters globally, which would probably result in different pruning rates for each layer. The following code illustrates one way to apply global pruning:

```
model = LeNet5().to(device)

parameters_to_prune = (
    (model.conv1, 'weight'),
```

```
        (model.conv2, 'weight'),
        (model.fc1, 'weight'),
        (model.fc2, 'weight'),
        (model.fc3, 'weight'),
)

prune.global_unstructured(
    parameters_to_prune,
    pruning_method=prune.L1Unstructured,
    amount=0.25)
```

Here we prune 25% of all the parameters in the entire model.

Pruning API

PyTorch provides built-in support for pruning in its
torch.nn.utils.prune module. Table 6-2 lists the available
functions in the pruning API.

Table 6-2. Pruning functions

Function	Description
is_pruned(*module*)	Checks whether the module is pruned
remove(*module*, *name*)	Removes the pruning reparameterization from a module and the pruning method from the forward hook
custom_from_mask(*module*, *name*, *mask*)	Prunes the tensor corresponding to the parameter called name in module by applying the precomputed mask in mask
global_unstructured(*params*, *pruning_method*)	Globally prunes tensors corresponding to all parameters in params by applying the specified pruning_method

Function	Description
`ln_structured(module, name, amount, n, dim)`	Prunes the tensor corresponding to the parameter called name in module by removing the specified amount of (currently unpruned) channels along the specified dim with the lowest Ln-norm
`random_structured(module, name, amount, dim)`	Prunes the tensor corresponding to the parameter called name in module by removing the specified amount of (currently unpruned) channels along the specified dim selected at random
`l1_unstructured(module, name, amount)`	Prunes the tensor corresponding to the parameter called name in module by removing the specified amount of (currently unpruned) units with the lowest L1-norm
`random_unstructured(module, name, amount)`	Prunes tensor corresponding to the parameter called name in module by removing the specified amount of (currently unpruned) units selected at random

Custom pruning methods

If you can't find a pruning method that suits your needs, you can create your own pruning method. To do so, create a subclass from the BasePruningMethod class provided in torch.nn.utils.prune. In most cases, you can leave the call(), apply_mask(), apply(), prune(), and remove() methods as they are.

However, you will need to write your own __init__() constructor and `compute_mask()` method to describe how your pruning method computes the mask. In addition, you'll need to specify the type of pruning (structured, unstructured, or global). The following code shows an example:

```
class MyPruningMethod(prune.BasePruningMethod):
  PRUNING_TYPE = 'unstructured'

  def compute_mask(self, t, default_mask):
    mask = default_mask.clone()
    mask.view(-1)[::2] = 0
    return mask

def my_unstructured(module, name):
  MyPruningMethod.apply(module, name)
  return module
```

First we define the class. This example prunes every other parameter, as defined by the code in `compute_mask()`. The PRUNING_TYPE is used to configure the pruning type as unstructured. Then we include and apply a function that instantiates the method. You would apply this pruning to your model in the following way:

```
model = LeNet5().to(device)
my_unstructured(model.fc1, name='bias')
```

You've now created your own custom pruning method and can apply it locally or globally.

This chapter showed you how to accelerate your training and optimize your models using PyTorch. The next step is to deploy your models and innovations into the world. In the next chapter, you'll learn how to deploy your models to the cloud and to mobile and edge devices, and I'll provide some reference code to build quick applications to showcase your designs.

## CHAPTER 7

Deploying PyTorch to Production

Most of this book so far has focused on model design and training. Earlier chapters showed you how to use the built-in capabilities of PyTorch to design your models and create custom NN modules, loss functions, optimizers, and other algorithms. In the previous chapter, we looked at how to use distributed training and model optimizations to accelerate your model training times and minimize the resources needed for running your models.

At this point, you have everything you need to create some well-trained, cutting-edge NN models—but don't let your innovations sit in isolation. Now it's time to deploy your models into the world through applications.

In the past, going from research to production was a challenging task that required a team of software engineers to move PyTorch models to a framework and integrate them into a (often non-Python) production environment. Today, PyTorch includes built-in tools and external libraries to support rapid deployment to a variety of production environments.

In this chapter, we focus on deploying your model for inference, not training, and we'll explore how to deploy your trained PyTorch models into a variety of applications. First, I'll describe the various built-in capabilities and tools within

PyTorch that you can use for deployment. Tools like Torch-Serve and TorchScript allow you to easily deploy your PyTorch models to the cloud and to mobile or edge devices.

Depending on the application and environment, you may have several options for deployment, each with its own trade-offs. I'll show you examples of how you can deploy your PyTorch models in multiple cloud and edge environments. You'll learn how to deploy to web servers for development and production at scale, to iOS and Android mobile devices, and to Internet of Things (IoT) devices based on ARM processors, GPUs, and field-programmable gate array (FPGA) hardware.

The chapter will also provide reference code, including references to the key APIs and libraries we use, to make getting started easy. When it comes time to deploy your models, you can refer back to this chapter for a quick reference so you can demonstrate your applications in cloud or mobile environments.

Let's begin by reviewing the resources that PyTorch provides to assist you in deploying your models.

PyTorch Deployment Tools and Libraries

PyTorch includes built-in tools and capabilities to facilitate deploying your model to production environments and edge devices. In this section, we'll explore those tools, and in the rest of the chapter we'll apply them to various environments.

PyTorch's deployment capabilities include its natural Python API, as well as the TorchServe, TorchScript, ONNX, and mobile libraries. Since PyTorch's natural API is Python-based, PyTorch models can be deployed as is in any environment that supports Python.

Table 7-1 summarizes the various resources available for deployment and indicates how to appropriately use each one.

Table 7-1. PyTorch resources for deployment

Resource	Use
Python API	Perform fast prototyping, training, and experimentation; program Python runtimes.
TorchScript	Improve performance and portability (e.g., load and run a model in C++); program non-Python runtimes or strict latency and performance requirements.
TorchServe	A fast production environment tool with model store, A/B testing, monitoring, and RESTful API.
ONNX	Deploy to systems with ONNX runtimes or FPGA devices.
Mobile libraries	Deploy to iOS and Android devices.

The following sections provide a reference and some sample code for each deployment resource. In each case, we'll use the same example model, described next.

Common Example Model

For each of the deployment resource examples and applications, as well as the reference code provided in this chapter, we will use the same model. For our examples, we'll deploy an image classifier using a VGG16 model pretrained with Image-Net data. That way, each section can focus on the deployment approach used and not the model itself. For each approach, you can replace the VGG16 model with one of your own and follow the same workflow to achieve results with your own designs.

The following code instantiates the model for use throughout this chapter:

```
from torchvision.models import vgg16

model = vgg16(pretrained=True)
```

We've used the VGG16 model before. To give you an idea of the model's complexity, let's print out the number of trainable parameters using the following code:

```python
import numpy as np

model_parameters = filter(lambda p:
    p.requires_grad, model.parameters())

params = sum([np.prod(p.size()) for
    p in model_parameters])
print(params)

# out: 138357544
```

The VGG16 model has 138,357,544 trainable parameters. As we go through each approach, keep in mind the performance at this level of complexity. You can use this as a rough benchmark when comparing the complexity of your models.

After we instantiate the VGG16 model, it requires minimal effort to deploy it in a Python application. In fact, we've already done this when we tested our models in previous chapters. Let's review the process one more time before we jump into other approaches.

Python API

The Python API is not a new resource. It's the same one we've been using throughout the book. I mention it here to point out that you can deploy your PyTorch models without any changes to your code. In this case, you simply call your model in evaluation mode with your desired inputs from any Python application, as shown in the following code:

```python
import system
import torch

if __name__ == "__main__":
    model = MyModel()
    model.load_state_dict(torch.load(PATH))
    model.eval()
    outputs = model(inputs)
    print(outputs)
```

The code loads the model, passes in the input, and prints out the output. This is a simple standalone Python application. You'll see how to deploy a model to a Python web server using a RESTful API and Flask later in this chapter. Using a Flask web server, you can build a quick browser application that demonstrates your model's capability.

Python is not always used in production environments due to its slower performance and lack of true multithreading. If your production environment uses another language (e.g., C++, Java, Rust, or Go), you can convert your models to TorchScript code.

TorchScript

TorchScript is a way to serialize and optimize your PyTorch model code so that your PyTorch models can be saved and executed in non-Python runtime environments with no dependency on Python. TorchScript is commonly used to run PyTorch models in C++ and with any language that supports C++ bindings.

TorchScript represents a PyTorch model in a format that can be understood, compiled, and serialized by the TorchScript compiler. The TorchScript compiler creates a serialized, optimized version of your model that can be used in C++ applications. To load your TorchScript model in C++, you would use the PyTorch C++ API library called *LibTorch*.

There are two ways to convert your PyTorch models to TorchScript. The first one is called *tracing*, which is a process in which you pass in an example input and perform the conversion with one line of code. It's used in most cases. The second is called *scripting*, and it's used when your model has more complex control code. For example, if your model has conditional if statements that depend on the input itself, you'll want to use scripting. Let's take a look at some reference code for each case.

Since our VGG16 example model does not have any control flow, we can use tracing to convert our model to TorchScript, as shown in the following code:

```
import torch

model = vgg16(pretrained=True)
example_input = torch.rand(1, 3, 224, 224)
torchscript_model = torch.jit.trace(model,
                                    example_input)
torchscript_model.save("traced_vgg16_model.pt")
```

The code creates a Python callable model, `torchscript_model`, that can be evaluated using a normal PyTorch approach such as `output = torchscript_model(inputs)`. Once we save the model, we can use it in a C++ application.

NOTE

The "normal" method of evaluating a model in PyTorch is often called `eager` mode since it's the quickest way to evaluate your models for development.

If our model used control flow, we would need to use the annotation method to convert it to TorchScript. Let's consider the following model:

```
import torch.nn as nn

class ControlFlowModel(nn.Module):
  def __init__(self, N):
    super(ControlFlowModel, self).__init__()
    self.fc = nn.Linear(N,100)

  def forward(self, input):
    if input.sum() > 0:
      output = input
    else:
      output = -input
    return output

model = ControlFlowModel(10)
```

```
torchcript_model = torch.jit.script(model)
torchscript_model.save("scripted_vgg16_model.pt")
```

In this example, the ControlFlowModel outputs and weights depend on the input values. In this case, we need to use torch.jit.script(), and then we can save the model to Torch-Script just like we did with tracing.

Now we can use our model in a C++ application, as shown in the following C++ code:

```cpp
include <torch/script.h>

#include <iostream>
#include <memory>

int main(int argc, const char* argv[]) {
  if (argc != 2) {
    std::cerr << "usage: example-app" >> \
      "<path-to-exported-script-module>\n";
    return -1;
  }

  torch::jit::script::Module model;
  model = torch::jit::load(argv[1]);

  std::vector<torch::jit::IValue> inputs;
  inputs.push_back( \
      torch::ones({1, 3, 224, 224}));

  at::Tensor output = model.forward(inputs).toTensor();
  std::cout \
    << output.slice(/*dim=*/1, \
        /*start=*/0, /*end=*/5) \
    << '\n';
  }

}
```

We pass in the filename of the TorchScript module to the program and load the model using torch::jit::load(). Then we create a sample input vector, run it through our TorchScript model, and convert the outputs to tensors, printing them to stdout.

The TorchScript API provides additional functions to support converting your models to TorchScript. Table 7-2 lists the supported functions.

Table 7-2. TorchScript API functions

Function	Description
`script(obj[, optimize, _frames_up, _rcb])`	Inspects the source code, compiles it as *TorchScript* code using the *TorchScript* compiler, and returns a `ScriptModule` or `Script Function`
`trace(func, example_inputs[, optimize, ...])`	Traces a function and returns an executable or `ScriptFunction` that will be optimized using just-in-time compilation
`script_if_tracing(fn)`	Compiles `fn` when it is first called during tracing
`trace_module(mod, inputs[, optimize, ...])`	Traces a module and returns an executable `ScriptModule` that will be optimized using just-in-time compilation
`fork(func, *args, **kwargs)`	Creates an asynchronous task executing `func` and a reference to the value of the result of this execution
`wait(future)`	Forces the completion of a `torch.jit.Future[T]` asynchronous task, returning the result of the task
`ScriptModule()`	Wraps a script into a C++ `torch::jit::Module`
`ScriptFunction()`	Works the same as `ScriptModule()` but represents a single function and does not have any attributes or parameters

Function	Description
`freeze(mod[, pre served_attrs])`	Clones a `ScriptModule` and attempts to inline the cloned module's submodules, parameters, and attributes as constants in the *TorchScript* IR Graph
`save(m, f[, _extra_files])`	Saves an offline version of the module for use in a separate process
`load(f[, map_location, _extra_files])`	Loads a `ScriptModule` or `ScriptFunction` previously saved with `torch.jit.save()`
`ignore([drop])`	Indicates to the compiler that a function or method should be ignored and left as a Python function
`unused(fn)`	Indicates to the compiler that a function or method should be ignored and replaced with the raising of an exception
`isinstance(obj, target_type)`	Provides for container-type refinement in TorchScript

In this section, we used TorchScript to increase the performance of our model when it's used in a C++ application or in a language that binds to C++. However, deploying PyTorch models at scale requires additional capabilities, like packaging models, configuring runtime environments, exposing API endpoints, logging and monitoring, and managing multiple model versions. Fortunately, PyTorch provides a tool called TorchServe to facilitate these tasks and rapidly deploy your models for inference at scale.

TorchServe

TorchServe is an open-source model-serving framework that makes it easy to deploy trained PyTorch models. It was developed by AWS engineers and jointly released with Facebook in April 2020, and it is actively maintained by AWS. TorchServe supports all the features needed to deploy models to production at scale, including multimodel serving, model versioning for A/B testing, logging and metrics for monitoring, and a RESTful API for integration with other systems. Figure 7-1 illustrates how TorchServe works.

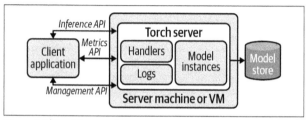

Figure 7-1. TorchServe architecture

The client application interfaces with TorchServe through multiple APIs. The Inference API provides the main inference requests and predictions. The client application sends input data through the RESTful API request and receives the prediction results. The Management API allows you to register and manage your deployed models. You can register, unregister, set default models, configure A/B testing, check status, and specify the number of workers for a model. The Metrics API allows you to monitor each model's performance.

TorchServe runs all model instances and captures server logs. It processes the frontend APIs and manages the model storage to disk. TorchServe also provides a number of default handlers for common applications like object detection and text classification. The handlers take care of converting data from the API into a format that your model will process. This helps speed up deployment since you don't have to write custom code for these common applications.

WARNING

TorchServe is experimental and subject to change.

To deploy your models via TorchServe, you will need to follow a few steps. First you need to install TorchServe's tools. Then you'll package your model using the model archiver tool. Once your models are archived, you'll then run the TorchServe web server. Once the web server is running, you can use its APIs to request predictions, manage your models, perform monitoring, or access server logs. Let's take a look at how to perform each step.

Install TorchServe and torch-model-archiver

AWS provides preinstalled machines with TorchServe in Amazon SageMaker or Amazon EC2 instances. If you're using a different cloud provider, check with them to see if preinstalled instances exist before getting started. If you're using a local server or need to install TorchServe, see the TorchServe installation instructions (*https://pytorch.tips/torchserve-install*).

A simple approach to try is to install with conda or pip, as shown in the following command lines:

```
$ conda install torchserve torch-model-archiver -c pytorch
```

```
$ pip install torchserve torch-model-archiver
```

If you run into issues, refer to the TorchServe installation instructions at the preceding link.

Package a model archive

TorchServe has the ability to package all model artifacts into a single-model archive file. To do so, we will use the torch-model-archiver command-line tool that we installed in the previous step. It packages model checkpoints as well as the state_dict into a *.mar* file that the TorchServe server uses to serve the model.

You can use the torch-model-archiver to archive your Torch-Script models as well as the standard "eager-mode" implementations, as shown in the following code.

For a TorchScript moel, the command line is as follows:

```
$ torch-model-archiver --model-name vgg16
  --version 1.0 --serialized-file model.pt --handler
  image_classifier
```

We set the model as our example VGG16 model and use the saved serialized file, *model.pt*. In this case, we can use the default image_classifier handler as well.

For the standard eager-mode model we would use the following command:

```
$ torch-model-archiver --model-name vgg16
  --version 1.0 --model-file model.py --serialized-file model.pt
  --handler image_classifier
```

This is similar to the previous command, but we also need to specify the model file, *model.py*.

The complete set of options for the torch-model-archiver tool is shown in the following code:

```
$ torch-model-archiver -h
usage: torch-model-archiver [-h]
        --model-name MODEL_NAME
        --version MODEL_VERSION_NUMBER
        --model-file MODEL_FILE_PATH
        --serialized-file MODEL_SERIALIZED_PATH
        --handler HANDLER
        [--runtime {python,python2,python3}]
        [--export-path EXPORT_PATH] [-f]
        [--requirements-file]
```

Table 7-3. Model archiver tool options

Options	Description
-h, --help	Help message. After the help message is displayed, the program will exit.
--model-name *MODEL_NAME*	Exported model name. Exported file will be named as *<model-name>.mar* and saved in the current working directory if no --export-path is specified, else it will be saved under the export path.
--serialized-file *SERIALIZED_FILE*	Path to a _.pt_ or _.pth_ file containing state_dict in case of eager mode or an executable ScriptModule in case of TorchScript.
--model-file *MODEL_FILE*	Path to Python file containing the model architecture. This parameter is mandatory for eager-mode models. The model architecture file must contain only one class definition extended from torch.nn.modules.
--handler *HANDLER*	*TorchServe*'s default handler name or Python file path to handle custom *TorchServe* inference logic.
--extra-files *EXTRA_FILES*	Comma-separated path to extra dependency files.
--runtime *{python, python2, python3}*	The runtime specifies which language to run your inference code on. The default runtime is RuntimeType.PYTHON, but at present the following runtimes are supported: python, python2, and python3.
--export-path *EXPORT_PATH*	Path where the exported _.mar_ file will be saved. This is an optional parameter. If --export-path is not specified, the file will be saved in the current working directory.

Options	Description
`--archive-format {tgz, no-archive, default}`	The format in which the model artifacts are archived. `tgz` creates the model archive in *<model-name>.tar.gz* format. If platform hosting requires model artifacts to be in *.tar.gz*, use this option. `no-archive` creates a nonarchived version of model artifacts at *<export-path>/<model-name>*. As a result of this choice, a MANIFEST file will be created at that location without archiving these model files. `default` creates the model archive in *<model-name>.mar* format. This is the default archiving format. Models archived in this format will be readily hostable on *TorchServe*.
`-f,--force`	When the `-f` or `--force` flag is specified, an existing *.mar* file with the same name as that provided in `--model-name` in the path specified by `--export-path` will be overwritten.
`-v, --version`	Model's version.
`-r, --requirements-file`	Path to a *requirements.txt* file containing a list of model-specific Python packages to be installed by *TorchServe* for seamless model serving.

We can save our model archive *.mar* file in the */models* folder. We'll use this as our model store. Next, let's run the TorchServe web server.

Run TorchServe

TorchServe includes a built-in web server that is run from the command line. It wraps one or more PyTorch models in a set of REST APIs and provides controls for configuring the port, host, and logging. The following command starts the web server with all models in the model store located in the */models* folder:

```
$ torchserve --model-store /models --start
  --models all
```

A complete set of options is shown in Table 7-4.

Table 7-4. TorchServe options

Options	Description
--model-store +*MODEL_STORE* + +*(mandatory)*+	Specifies the model store location where models can be loaded
-h, --help	Shows the help message and exits
-v, --version	Returns the TorchServe version
--start	Starts the model server
--stop	Stops the model server
--ts-config +*TS_CONFIG*+	Indicates the configuration file for TorchServe
--models +*MODEL_PATH1* *MODEL_NAME=MODEL_PATH2...* [*MODEL_PATH1* *MODEL_NAME=MODEL_PATH2...* ...]+	Indicates the models to be loaded using `[model_name=]model_location` format; locations can be an HTTP URL, a model archive file, or a directory that contains model archive files in `MODEL_STORE`
--log-config +*LOG_CONFIG*+	Indicates the log4j configuration file for TorchServe
--ncs, --no-config-snapshots	Disables the snapshot feature

Now that the TorchServe web server is running, you can use the Inference API to send data and request predictions.

Request predictions

You use the Inference API to pass data and request predictions. The Inference API listens on port 8080 and is only accessible from localhost by default. To change the default setting, refer to the TorchServe documentation (*https://pytorch.org/serve/config uration.html*). To get predictions from the server, we use the

Inference API's `Service.Predictions` gRPC API and make a REST call to */predictions/<model_name>*, as shown using `curl` in the following command line:

```
$curl http://localhost:8080/predictions/vgg16
  -T hot_dog.jpg
```

The code assumes we have an image file, *hot_dog.jpg*. The JSON-formatted response would look something like this:

```
{
    "class": "n02175045 hot dog",
    "probability": 0.788482002828
}
```

You can also use the Inference API to do a health check using the following request:

```
$ curl http://localhost:8080/ping
```

The response will look like the following if the server is running:

```
{
  "health": "healthy!"
}
```

For a full list of inference APIs use the following command:

```
$ curl -X OPTIONS http://localhost:8080
```

Logging and monitoring

You can configure metrics using the Metrics API and monitor and log your models' performance when deployed. The Metrics API listens on port 8082 and is only accessible from localhost by default, but you can change the default when configuring your TorchServe server. The following command illustrates how to access metrics:

```
$ curl http://127.0.0.1:8082/metrics

# HELP ts_inference_latency_microseconds
#     Cumulative inference

# TYPE ts_inference_latency_microseconds counter
ts_inference_latency_microseconds{
  uuid="d5f84dfb-fae8-4f92-b217-2f385ca7470b",...
```

```
ts_inference_latency_microseconds{
  uuid="d5f84dfb-fae8-4f92-b217-2f385ca7470b",model_name="noop"...

# HELP ts_inference_requests_total Total number of inference ...

# TYPE ts_inference_requests_total counter
ts_inference_requests_total{
  uuid="d5f84dfb-fae8-4f92-b217-2f385ca7470b",...
ts_inference_requests_total{
  uuid="d5f84dfb-fae8-4f92-b217-2f385ca7470b",model_name="noop"...

# HELP ts_queue_latency_microseconds Cumulative queue duration ...

# TYPE ts_queue_latency_microseconds counter
ts_queue_latency_microseconds{
  uuid="d5f84dfb-fae8-4f92-b217-2f385ca7470b",...
ts_queue_latency_microseconds{
  uuid="d5f84dfb-fae8-4f92-b217-2f385ca7470b",model_name="noop"...
```

The default metrics endpoint returns Prometheus-formatted metrics. Prometheus is a free software application used for event monitoring and alerting that records real-time metrics in a time series database built using an HTTP pull model. You can query metrics using curl requests or point a Prometheus Server to the endpoint and use Grafana for dashboards. See the Metrics API documentation (*https://pytorch.tips/serve-metrics*) for more details.

Metrics are logged to a file. TorchServe also supports other types of server logging, including access logs and TorchServe logs. Access logs record the inference requests and the time it takes to complete the requests. As defined in the *properties* file, the access logs are collected in the *<log_location>/access_log.log* file. TorchServe logs collect all the logs from TorchServe and its backend workers.

TorchServe supports capabilities beyond the default settings for metrics and logging. Metrics and logging can be configured in many different ways. In addition, you can create custom logs. For more information on metric and logging customization and other advanced features of TorchServe, refer to the Torch-Serve documentation (*https://pytorch.tips/torchserve*).

NOTE

The *NVIDIA Triton Inference Server* is becoming more popular and is also used to deploy AI models at scale in production. Although not part of the PyTorch project, you may want to consider the Triton Inference Server as an alternative to TorchServe, especially when deploying to NVIDIA GPUs.

The Triton Inference Server is open source software and can load models from local storage, GCP, or AWS S3. Triton supports running multiple models on single or multiple GPUs, low latency and shared memory, and model ensembles. Some possible advantages of Triton over TorchServe include:

- Triton is out of beta.
- It is the fastest way to infer on NVIDIA hardware (common).
- It can use `int4` quantization.
- You can port directly from PyTorch without ONNX.

Available as a Docker container, Triton Inference Server also integrates with Kubernetes for orchestration, metrics, and auto-scaling. For more information, visit the NVIDIA Triton Inference Server documentation (*https:// pytorch.tips/triton*).

ONNX

If your platform doesn't support PyTorch and you cannot use TorchScript/C++ or TorchServe for your deployment, it may be possible that your deployment platform supports the Open Neural Network Exchange (ONNX) format. The ONNX format defines a common set of operators and a common file format so that deep learning engineers can use models across a variety of frameworks, tools, runtimes, and compilers.

ONNX was developed by Facebook and Microsoft to allow model interoperability between PyTorch and other frameworks, such as Caffe2 and Microsoft Cognitive Toolkit (CTK). ONNX is currently supported by inference runtimes from a number of providers, including Cadence Systems, Habana, Intel AI, NVIDIA, Qualcomm, Tencent, Windows, and Xilinx.

An example use case is edge deployment on a Xilinx FPGA device. FPGA devices are custom chips that can be programmed with specific logic. They are used by edge devices for low-latency or high-performance applications, like video. If you want to deploy your new innovative model to an FPGA device, you would first convert it to ONNX format and then use the Xilinx FPGA development tools to generate an FPGA image with your model's implementation.

Let's take a look at an example of how to export a model to ONNX, again using our VGG16 model. The ONNX exporter can use tracing or scripting. We learned about tracing and scripting, described in the earlier section on TorchScript. We can use tracing by simply providing the model and an example input. The following code shows how we'd export our VGG16 model to ONNX using tracing:

```
model = vgg16(pretrained=True)
example_input = torch.rand(1, 3, 224, 224)
onnx_model = torch.onnx.export(model,
                               example_input,
                               "vgg16.onnx")
```

We define an example input and call `torch.onnx.export()`. The resulting file, *vgg16.onnx*, is a binary protobuf file that contains both the network structure and the parameters of the VGG16 model we exported.

If we want to verify that our model was converted to ONNX properly, we can use the ONNX checker, as shown in the following code:

```
import onnx

model = onnx.load("vgg16.onnx")
onnx.checker.check_model(model)
onnx.helper.printable_graph(model.graph)
```

This code uses the Python ONNX library to load the model, run the checker, and print out a human-readable version of the model. You may need to install the ONNX library before running the code, using conda or pip.

To learn more about converting to ONNX or running in an ONNX runtime, check out the ONNX tutorial (*https://pytorch.tips/onnx-tutorial*) on the PyTorch website.

In addition to TorchScript, TorchServe, and ONNX, more tools are being developed to support PyTorch model deployment. Let's consider some tools used to deploy models to mobile platforms.

Mobile Libraries

Android and iPhone devices are continuously evolving and adding native support for deep learning acceleration in their custom chipsets. In addition, there is a growing need to reduce latency, preserve privacy, and interact seamlessly with deep learning models in applications such as augmented reality (AR). Deployment to mobile devices is further complicated due to mobile runtimes that can significantly differ from the training environments used by developers, leading to errors and challenges during mobile deployment.

PyTorch Mobile addresses these challenges and provides an end-to-end workflow to go from training to mobile deployment. PyTorch Mobile is available for iOS, Android, and Linux and provides APIs for the preprocessing and integration tasks needed for mobile applications. The basic workflow is shown in Figure 7-2.

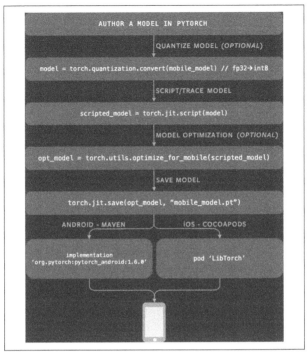

Figure 7-2. PyTorch mobile workflow

You start by designing your model in PyTorch as you normally would. Then you may quantize your model to reduce its complexity with minimal degradation in performance. Subsequently, you would use tracing or scripting to convert to TorchScript and optimize your model for mobile devices using `torch.utils`. Next, save your model and use the appropriate mobile library for deployment. Android uses the Maven PyTorch library and iOS uses CocoPods with the LibTorch pod.

For the latest details on PyTorch Mobile, refer to the PyTorch Mobile documentation (*https://pytorch.tips/mobile*).

Now that we've explored some PyTorch tools available for deploying our models, let's take a look at some reference applications and code for deployment to the cloud and to edge devices. First I'll show you how to build a web server for development using Flask.

Deploying to a Flask App

Before deploying to full-scale production, you may want to deploy your models to a development web server. This enables you to integrate your deep learning algorithms with other systems and quickly build prototypes to demonstrate your new models. One of the easiest ways to build a development server is with Python using Flask.

Flask is a simple micro web framework written in Python. It is called a "micro" framework because it does not include a database abstraction layer, form validation, upload handling, various authentication technologies, or anything else that might be provided with other libraries. We won't cover Flask in depth in this book, but I'll show you how to use Flask to deploy your models in Python.

We'll also expose a REST API so that other applications can pass in data and receive predictions. In the following examples, we'll deploy our pretrained VGG16 model and classify images. First we'll define our API endpoints, request types, and response types. Our API endpoint will be at */predict*, which takes in POST requests (including the image file). The response will be in JSON format and contain a class_id and class_name from the ImageNet dataset.

Let's create our main Flask file, called *app.py*. First we'll import the required packages:

```
import io
import json

from torchvision import models
import torchvision.transforms as transforms
from PIL import Image
from flask import Flask, jsonify, request
```

We'll be using io to convert bytes to an image and json to handle JSON-formatted data. We'll be using torchvision to create our VGG16 model and transform the image data into the appropriate format for our model. Finally, we import Flask, jsonnify, and request to handle the API requests and responses.

Before we create our web server, let's define a get_prediction() function that reads in image data, preprocesses it, passes it into our model, and returns the image class:

```
import json
imagenet_class_index = json.load(
    open("./imagenet_class_index.json"))

model = models.vgg16(pretrained=True)

image_transforms = transforms.Compose(
    [transforms.Resize(255),
     transforms.CenterCrop(224),
     transforms.ToTensor(),
     transforms.Normalize(
         [0.485, 0.456, 0.406],
         [0.229, 0.224, 0.225])])

def get_prediction(image_bytes):
    image = Image.open(io.BytesIO(image_bytes))
    tensor = image_transforms(image)
    outputs = model(tensor)
    _, y = outputs.max(1)
    predicted_idx = str(y.item())
    return imagenet_class_index[predicted_idx]
```

Since our model will return a number indicating the class, we'll need a lookup table to convert this number to a class name. We create a dictionary called `imagenet_class_index` by reading in the JSON conversion file. We then instantiate our VGG16 model and define our image transforms to preprocess a PIL image by resizing it, center-cropping it, converting it to a tensor, and normalizing it. These steps are required prior to sending the image into our model.

Our `get_prediction()` function creates a PIL image object based on the received bytes and applies the required image transforms to create an input tensor. Next, we perform the forward pass (or model inference) and find the class with highest probability, y. Last, we look up the class name using the output class value.

Now that we have code that preprocesses an image, passes it through our model, and returns the predicted class, we can create our Flask web server and endpoints and deploy our model, as shown in the following code:

```
app = Flask(__name__)

@app.route('/predict', methods=['POST'])
def predict():
  if request.method == 'POST':
    file = request.files['file']
  img_bytes = file.read()
  class_id, class_name = \
    get_prediction(image_bytes=img_bytes)
  return jsonify({'class_id': class_id,
                  'class_name': class_name})
```

Our web server object is called `app`. We've created it, but it's not running yet. We set our endpoint to */predict* and configured it to handle POST requests. When the web server receives the POST, it will execute the `predict()` function that reads the image, gets the prediction, and returns the image class in JSON format.

That's it! Now we just need to add the following code so that the web server runs when we execute *app.py*:

```
if __name__ == '__main__':
    app.run()
```

To test our web server, we can run it as follows:

```
>>> FLASK_ENV=development FLASK_APP=app.py flask run
```

We can send an image using a simple Python file and the requests library:

```
import requests

resp = requests.post(
    "http://localhost:5000/predict",
    files={"file": open('cat.jpg','rb')})

print(resp.json())

>>> {"class_id": "n02124075", "class_name": "Egyptian_cat"}
```

In this example, we're running a web server on our local machine on port 5000 (localhost:5000). You may want to run your development web server in Google Colab to take advantage of cloud GPUs. I'll show you how to do so next.

Colab Flask App

Perhaps you've been developing your PyTorch models in Colab to take advantage of its rapid development or its GPUs. Colab provides a virtual machine (VM) which routes its localhost to our machine's local host. To expose it to a public URL, we can use a library called ngrok.

First install ngrok in Colab:

```
!pip install flask-ngrok
```

To run our Flask app with ngrok, all we need to do is add two lines of code, as shown in the following annotations:

```
from flask_ngrok import run_with_ngrok    ❶

@app.route("/")
def home():
    return "<h1>Running Flask on Google Colab!</h1>"

app.run()
```

```
app = Flask(__name__)
run_with_ngrok(app)  ❷

@app.route('/predict', methods=['POST'])
def predict():
  if request.method == 'POST':
    file = request.files['file']
  img_bytes = file.read()
  class_id, class_name = \
    get_prediction(image_bytes=img_bytes)
  return jsonify({'class_id': class_id,
                  'class_name': class_name})

app.run()  ❸
```

❶   Import the ngrok library.

❷   Starts ngrok when the app is run.

❸   Since we're running in Colab, we don't need to check for main.

I've omitted the other imports and the get_prediction() function as they do not change. Now you can run your development web server in Colab for even faster prototyping. The ngrok library provides a secure URL for the server running in Colab; you'll find the URL in the Colab notebook output when running the Flask app. For example, the following output shows that the URL is *http://c0c97117ba27.ngrok.io*:

```
 * Serving Flask app "__main__" (lazy loading)
 * Environment: production
   WARNING: This is a development server.
     Do not use it in a production deployment.
   Use a production WSGI server instead.
 * Debug mode: off
 * Running on http://127.0.0.1:5000/ (Press CTRL+C to quit)
 * Running on http://c0c97117ba27.ngrok.io
 * Traffic stats available on http://127.0.0.1:4040
127.0.0.1 - - [08/Dec/2020 20:46:05] "GET / HTTP/1.1" 200 -
127.0.0.1 - - [08/Dec/2020 20:46:05]
  "GET /favicon.ico HTTP/1.1" 404 -
127.0.0.1 - - [08/Dec/2020 20:46:06] "GET / HTTP/1.1" 200 -
```

Once again, you can send a POST request with an image to test the web server. You can run the following code locally or in another Colab notebook:

```
import requests

resp = requests.post(
      "http://c0c97117ba27.ngrok.io/predict",
      files={"file": open('cat.jpg','rb')})

print(resp.json())

# out :
# {"class_id": "n02124075",
#  "class_name": "Egyptian_cat"}
```

Notice the URL has changed. Deploying your model in a Flask app is a good way to quickly test it and the get_prediction() function with a REST API. However, our Flask app here is used as a development web server, not for production deployment. When deploying your models at scale, you will need to address things like model management, A/B testing, monitoring, logging, and other tasks to ensure your model server is working properly. To deploy to production at scale, we'll use TorchServe.

Deploying to the Cloud with TorchServe

In this example, we'll deploy our VGG16 image classifier to a production environment. Let's pretend our company makes a software tool that will sort collections of retail product images into categories depending on which objects appear in the images. The company is growing rapidly and now supports millions of small businesses that use the tool daily.

As part of the machine learning engineering team, you'll need to deploy your model to production and provide a simple REST API that the software tool will use to classify its images. Because we want to deploy something as quickly as possible, we'll use a Docker container in an AWS EC2 instance.

Quick Start with Docker

TorchServe provides scripts to create Docker images based on a variety of platforms and options. Running a Docker container eliminates the need to reinstall all the dependencies required to run TorchServe. In addition, we can scale our model inference by spinning multiple Docker containers using Kubernetes. First we must create the Docker image according to the resources we have on our EC2 instance.

The first step is to clone the TorchServe repository and navigate to the *Docker* folder, using the following commands:

```
$ git clone https://github.com/pytorch/serve.git
cd serve/docker
```

Next we'll need to add our model archive for VGG16 into the Docker image. We do this by adding the following line to the Dockerfile that downloads the archived model file and saves it within the */home/model-server/* directory:

```
$ curl -o /home/model-server/vgg16.pth \
    https://download.pytorch.org/models/vgg16.pth
```

We can now run the *build_image.sh* script to create a Docker image with the public binaries installed. Since we're running on an EC2 instance with a GPU, we'll use the -g flag, as follows:

```
$ ./build_image.sh -g
```

You can run **./build_image.sh -h** to see additional options.

Once our Docker image is created, we can run the container with the following command:

```
$ docker run --rm -it --gpus '"device=1"' \
    -p 8080:8080 -p 8081:8081 -p 8082:8082 \
    -p 7070:7070 -p 7071:7071 \
    pytorch/torchserve:latest-gpu
```

This command will start the container with the 8080/81/82 and 7070/71 ports exposed to the outer world's localhost. It uses one GPU with the latest CUDA version.

Now our TorchServe Docker container is running. Our company's software tool can send inference requests by sending the image file to *ourip.com/predict* and can receive image classifications via JSON.

For more details on running TorchServe in Docker, refer to the TorchServe Docker documentation (*https://pytorch.tips/torchserve-docker*). To learn more about TorchServe, visit the TorchServe repository (*https://pytorch.tips/torchserve-github*).

Now you can deploy your models to your local machine and cloud servers using Flask for development or TorchServe for production. This is useful for prototyping and integrating with other applications through a REST API. Next, you'll expand your deployment capabilities outside of the cloud: in the following section we'll explore how you would deploy models to mobile devices and other edge devices.

Deploying to Mobile and Edge

Edge devices are (usually small) hardware systems that interface directly with the user or environment and run machine learning computations directly on the device instead of on a centralized server in the cloud. Some examples of edge devices include mobile phones and tablets, wearables like smart watches and heart rate monitors, and other IoT devices such as industrial sensors and home thermostats. There's a growing need to run deep learning algorithms on edge devices in order to maintain privacy, reduce data transfer, minimize latency, and support new interactive use cases in real time.

First we'll explore how to deploy your PyTorch models on mobile devices with iOS and Android, then we'll cover other edge devices. PyTorch's support for edge deployment is limited but growing. These sections will provide some reference code to help you get started using PyTorch Mobile.

iOS

According to Apple, as of January 2021 there were over 1.65 billion active iOS devices in the world. The support for machine learning hardware acceleration continues to grow with each new model and custom processing unit. Learning how to deploy your PyTorch models to iOS opens the doors for many opportunities to create an iOS app based on deep learning.

To deploy your model to an iOS device, you'll need to learn how to create an iOS application using development tools like Xcode. We won't cover iOS development in this book, but you can find a "Hello, World" program and sample code to help you build your app at the PyTorch iOS Example Apps GitHub repository (*https://pytorch.tips/ios-demo*).

Let's describe the workflow for deploying our VGG16 network to an iOS application. iOS will use the PyTorch C++ API to interface with our model, so we'll need to convert and save our model to TorchScript first. Then we'll wrap the C++ function in Objective-C so iOS Swift code can access the API. We'll use Swift to load and preprocess an image, and then we'll pass the image data into our model to predict its class.

First we will convert our VGG16 model to TorchScript using tracing and save it as *model.pt*, as shown in the following code:

```python
import torch
import torchvision
from torch.utils.mobile_optimizer \
  import optimize_for_mobile

model = torchvision.models.vgg16(pretrained=True)
model.eval()
example = torch.rand(1, 3, 224, 224)  ❶

traced_script_module = \
  torch.jit.trace(model, example)  ❷
torchscript_model_optimized = \
  optimize_for_mobile(traced_script_module)  ❸
torchscript_model_optimized.save("model.pt")  ❹
```

❶ Define example using random data.

❷ Convert model to TorchScript.

❸ New step to optimize the code.

❹ Save the model.

As described earlier, using tracing requires defining an example input, and we do so using random data. Then we convert the model to TorchScript using torch.jit.trace(). We then add a new step to optimize the TorchScript code for mobile platforms using the torch.utils.mobile_optimizer package. Finally, we save the model to a file named *model.pt*.

Now we'll need to write our Swift iOS application. Our iOS app will use the PyTorch C++ library, which we can install via CocoaPods as follows:

```
$ pod install
```

Then we need to write some Swift code to load a sample image. You can improve this in the future by accessing the camera or photos on the device, but for now we'll keep it simple:

```swift
let image = UIImage(named: "image.jpg")! \
  imageView.image = image

let resizedImage = image.resized(
  to: CGSize(width: 224, height: 224))

guard var pixelBuffer = resizedImage.normalized()
else return
```

Here we resize the image to 224 × 224 pixels and run a function to normalize the image data.

Next we load and instantiate our model into our iOS app, as shown in the following code:

```swift
private lazy var module: TorchModule = {
    if let filePath = Bundle.main.path(
      forResource: "model", ofType: "pt"),

        let module = TorchModule(
```

```
                    fileAtPath: filePath) {
            return module
        } else {
            fatalError("Can't find the model file!")
        }
    }()
```

iOS is written in Swift, and Swift cannot interface to C++, so we need to use an Objective-C class, TorchModule, as a wrapper for torch::jit::script::Module.

Now that our model is loaded, we can predict an image's class by passing the preprocessed image data into our model and running a prediction, as shown in the following code:

```
guard let outputs = module.predict(image:
  UnsafeMutableRawPointer(&pixelBuffer))
else {
    return
}
```

Under the hood, the predict() Objective-C wrapper calls the C++ forward() function as follows:

```
at::Tensor tensor = torch::from_blob(
  imageBuffer, {1, 3, 224, 224}, at::kFloat);

torch::autograd::AutoGradMode guard(false);
auto outputTensor = _impl.forward(
  {tensor}).toTensor();
float* floatBuffer =
  outputTensor.data_ptr<float>();
```

When you run the sample app, you should see output similar to Figure 7-3 for the sample image file.

This image classification example is only a small representation of the capabilities of coding for iOS devices. For more advanced use cases, you can still follow the same process: convert and save to TorchScript, create an Objective-C wrapper, preprocess the input, and call your predict() function. Next, we'll follow a similar process for deploying PyTorch to Android mobile devices.

- white wolf, Arctic wolf, Canis lupus tundrarum

- timber wolf, grey wolf, gray wolf, Canis lupus

- Eskimo dog, husky

Figure 7-3. iOS example

Android

Android mobile devices are also abundantly used throughout the world, with the OS estimated to have a market share of over 70% in mobile devices at the start of 2021. This means there is also a huge opportunity to deploy PyTorch models to Android devices.

Android uses the PyTorch Android API, and you will need to install the Android development tools to build a sample app. Using Android Studio, you will be able to install the Android native development kit (NDK) and software development kit (SDK). We won't cover Android development in the book, but you can find a "Hello, World" program and sample code to help you build your app at the PyTorch Android Example GitHub repository (*https://pytorch.tips/android-demo*).

The workflow for deploying a PyTorch model on an Android device is very similar to the process we used for iOS. We'll still need to convert our model to TorchScript to use it with the PyTorch Android API. However, since the API natively supports loading and running our TorchScript model, we do not need to wrap it in C++ code as we did with iOS. Instead, we'll use Java to write an Android app that loads and preprocesses an image file, passes it to our model for inference, and returns the results.

Let's deploy our VGG16 model to Android. First we convert the model to TorchScript just like we did for iOS, as shown in the following code:

```python
import torch
import torchvision
from torch.utils.mobile_optimizer \
  import optimize_for_mobile

model = torchvision.models.vgg16(pretrained=True)
model.eval()
example = torch.rand(1, 3, 224, 224)

traced_script_module = \
  torch.jit.trace(model, example)
torchscript_model_optimized = \
  optimize_for_mobile(traced_script_module)
torchscript_model_optimized.save("model.pt")
```

We convert the model to TorchScript using tracing with `torch.jit.trace()`. We then add a new step to optimize the TorchScript code for mobile platforms using the `torch.utils.mobile_optimizer` package. Finally, we save the model to a file named *model.pt*.

Next, we create our Android app using Java. We add the PyTorch Android API to our app as a Gradle dependency by adding the following code to *build.gradle*:

```
repositories {
  jcenter()
}

dependencies {
  implementation
    'org.pytorch:pytorch_android:1.4.0'
  implementation
    'org.pytorch:pytorch_android_torchvision:1.4.0'
}
```

Next, we write our Android app. We start by loading an image and preprocessing it with the following code:

```
Bitmap bitmap = \
  BitmapFactory.decodeStream(
    getAssets().open("image.jpg"));

Tensor inputTensor = \
  TensorImageUtils.bitmapToFloat32Tensor(
    bitmap,
    TensorImageUtils.TORCHVISION_NORM_MEAN_RGB,
    TensorImageUtils.TORCHVISION_NORM_STD_RGB);
```

Now that we have our image, we can predict its class, but first we must load our model, as follows:

```
Module module = Module.load(
  assetFilePath(this, "model.pt"));
```

Then we can run inference to predict the image's class and process the results with the following code:

```
Tensor outputTensor = module.forward(
  IValue.from(inputTensor)).toTensor();
float[] scores = \
  outputTensor.getDataAsFloatArray();

float maxScore = -Float.MAX_VALUE;
int maxScoreIdx = -1;
for (int i = 0; i < scores.length; i++) {
  if (scores[i] > maxScore) {
    maxScore = scores[i];
    maxScoreIdx = i;
  }
```

```
    }
    String className = \
        ImageNetClasses.IMAGENET_CLASSES[maxScoreIdx];
```

This workflow can be used for more advanced use cases. You can use the camera or photos on the device or other Android sensors to create more complex apps. For more PyTorch Android demo applications, visit the PyTorch Android Demo App GitHub repository (*https://pytorch.tips/android-demo-repo*).

Other Edge Devices

Mobile devices running iOS or Android represent one type of edge device, but there are many more that can execute deep learning algorithms. Edge devices are often built using custom hardware for a specific application. Examples of other edge devices include sensors, video equipment, medical monitors, software-defined radios, thermostats, farming machines, and manufacturing sensors to detect defects.

Most edge devices include computer processors, GPUs, FPGAs, or other custom ASIC computer chips that are capable of running deep learning models. So how do you deploy your PyTorch models to these edge devices? Well, it depends on what processing components are used on the device. Let's explore some ideas for commonly used chips:

CPUs

If your edge device uses a CPU, such as an Intel or AMD processor, PyTorch can be deployed in Python and C++ using both TorchScript and the C++ frontend API. Mobile and edge CPU chipsets are usually optimized to minimize power, and memory may be more limited on an edge device. It may be worthwhile to optimize your models using pruning or quantization prior to deployment to minimize the power and memory required to run inference.

ARMs

ARM processors are a family of computer processors with a reduced set of instructions. They typically run at lower power and clock speeds than Intel or AMD CPUs and can be included within Systems on a Chip (SoCs). In addition to the processor, SoCs chips usually include other electronics such as programmable FPGA logic or GPUs. Running PyTorch in Linux on ARM devices is currently under development.

Microcontrollers

Microcontrollers are very limited processors that are usually aimed at very simple control tasks. Some popular microcontrollers include Arduino and Beaglebone processors. Support for microcontrollers is limited due to the few resources available.

GPUs

Edge devices may include GPU chips. NVIDIA GPUs, are the most widely supported GPUs, but other companies (such as AMD and Intel) manufacture GPU chips as well. NVIDIA supports PyTorch in its GPU development kits, including its Jetson Nano, Xavier, and NX boards.

FPGAs

PyTorch models can be deployed to many FPGA devices, including Xilinx (recently acquired by AMD) and Intel FPGA device families. Neither platform supports direct PyTorch deployment; however, they do support the ONNX format. The typical approach is to convert PyTorch models to ONNX and use the FPGA development tools to create FPGA logic from the ONNX model.

TPUs

Google's TPU chips are being deployed across edge devices as well. PyTorch is supported via the XLA library, as described in "PyTorch on a TPU" on page 156. Deploying your models to edge devices that utilize TPUs can enable you to run inference using the XLA library.

ASICs

Many companies are developing their own custom chips or ASICs that implement model designs in a highly optimized and efficient manner. The ability to deploy your PyTorch models will depend heavily on the capabilities supported by the custom ASIC chip designs and development tools. In some cases, you may be able to use the PyTorch/XLA library if the ASIC supports it.

When it comes time to deploy your PyTorch models to an edge device, consider the processing components available on the system. Depending on the chips available, investigate your options to utilize the C++ frontend API, leverage TorchScript, convert your models to ONNX format, or access the PyTorch XLA library to deploy your models.

In this chapter, you learned how to use the standard Python API, TorchScript/C++, TorchServe, ONNX, and the PyTorch mobile libraries to deploy your models for inference. The chapter also provided reference code to deploy your PyTorch models to local development servers or production environments in the cloud using Flask and TorchServe, as well as to iOS and Android devices.

PyTorch supports a large, active ecosystem of useful tools for model development and deployment. We'll explore this ecosystem in the next chapter, which also provides reference code for some of the most popular PyTorch tools.

## CHAPTER 8

The PyTorch Ecosystem and Additional Resources

In the previous chapters, you've learned everything you need to design and deploy deep learning models with PyTorch. You have learned how to build, train, test, and accelerate your models across different platforms and how to deploy those models to the cloud and edge devices. As you've seen, PyTorch has powerful capabilities in both development and deployment environments and is highly extensible, allowing you to create customizations tailored to your needs.

To conclude this reference guide, we'll explore the PyTorch Ecosystem, other supporting libraries, and additional resources. The PyTorch Ecosystem is one of the most powerful advantages of PyTorch. It provides a rich set of projects, tools, models, libraries, and platforms to explore AI and accelerate your AI development.

The PyTorch Ecosystem includes projects and libraries created by researchers, third-party vendors, and the PyTorch community. These projects are well maintained and have been vetted by the PyTorch team to ensure their quality and utility.

In addition, the PyTorch project includes other libraries that support specific domains, including Torchvision for computer vision and Torchtext for NLP. PyTorch also supports other packages like TensorBoard for visualization, and there's an abundance of learning resources for further study, like Papers with Code and PyTorch Academy.

In this chapter, we'll begin with an overview of the PyTorch Ecosystem and a high-level view of its supported projects and tools. Then we'll dig a little deeper into some of the most powerful and popular resources, with reference material about their usage and APIs provided along the way. Finally, I'll show you how to learn more with a variety of tutorials, books, courses, and other training resources.

Let's start by looking at all the Ecosystem has to offer.

The PyTorch Ecosystem

As of early 2021, the PyTorch Ecosystem (*https://pytorch.tips/ ecosystem*) features over 50 libraries and projects, and the list continues to grow. Some of these are domain-specific projects, such as those specifically for computer vision or NLP solutions. Other projects, such as PyTorch Lightning and fastai, provide frameworks for writing concise code, while projects like PySyft and Crypten support security and privacy. There are also projects that support reinforcement learning, gaming models, model interpretability, and acceleration. In this section, we'll explore projects included in the PyTorch Ecosystem.

Table 8-1 provides a list of the Ecosystem projects that support *computer vision* applications.

Table 8-1. Computer vision projects

Project	Description
Torchvision	PyTorch's computer vision library that provides common transforms, models, and utilities to support computer vision applications (*https://pytorch.tips/torchvision*)
Detectron2	Facebook's objection detection and segmentation platform (*https://pytorch.tips/detectron2*)

Project	Description
Albumentations	Image augmentation library (*https://pytorch.tips/albumentations*)
PyTorch3D	Collection of reusable components for 3D computer vision (*https://pytorch.tips/pytorch3d*)
Kornia	Library of differentiable modules for computer vision (*https://pytorch.tips/kornia*)
MONAI	Framework for deep learning in healthcare imaging (*https://pytorch.tips/monai*)
TorchIO	Toolkit for 3D medical images (*https://pytorch.tips/torchio*)

Torchvision is one of the most powerful libraries for computer vision applications and is included in the PyTorch project. It's also maintained by the PyTorch development team. We'll cover the Torchvision API in more detail later in this chapter.

PyTorch3D and TorchIO provide additional support for 3D imaging, while TorchIO and MONAI focus on medical imaging applications. Detectron2 is a powerful platform for object detection. If you're conducting computer vision research and development, these extensions may help accelerate your results.

As with computer vision, there have been major advances in NLP research over the past decade, and NLP applications are also well supported by PyTorch.

Table 8-2 provides a list of the Ecosystem projects that support *NLP and audio-based* applications.

Table 8-2. NLP and audio projects

Project	Description
Torchtext	PyTorch's NLP and text processing library (*https://pytorch.tips/torchtext*)
Flair	Simple framework for NLP (*https://pytorch.tips/flair*)
AllenNLP	Library for designing and evaluating NLP models (*https://pytorch.tips/allennlp*)

Project	Description
ParlAI	Framework for sharing, training, and testing dialogue models (*https://pytorch.tips/parlai*)
NeMo	Toolkit for conversational AI (*https://pytorch.tips/nemo*)
PyTorch NLP	Basic utilities for NLP (*https://pytorch.tips/pytorchnlp*)
Translate	Facebook's machine translation platform (*https://pytorch.tips/translate*)
TorchAudio	PyTorch's library for audio preprocessing (*https://pytorch.tips/torchaudio*)

Like Torchvision, Torchtext is included as part of the PyTorch project and is maintained by the PyTorch development team. Torchtext provides powerful functionality for processing text data and developing NLP-based models.

Flair, AllenNLP, and PyTorch NLP provide additional capabilities for text-based processing and NLP model development. ParlAI and NeMo provide tools to develop dialogue and conversational AI systems, while Translate focuses on machine translation.

TorchAudio provides functions for handling audio files like speech and music.

Reinforcement learning and gaming are also rapidly growing fields of research, and there are tools to support them using PyTorch.

Table 8-3 provides a list of the Ecosystem projects that support *gaming and reinforcement learning* applications.

Table 8-3. Gaming and reinforcement learning projects

Project	Description
ELF	Project for training and testing algorithms in game environments (*https://pytorch.tips/elf*)
PFRL	Library of deep reinforcement algorithms (*https://pytorch.tips/pfrl*)

ELF (extensive, lightweight, and flexible platform for game research) is an open source project developed by Facebook that reimplements gaming algorithms like AlphaGoZero and AlphaZero. PFRL (preferred reinforcement learning) is a PyTorch-based open source deep reinforcement learning library developed by Preferred Networks, the creators of Chainer and ChainerRL. It can be used to create baseline algorithms for reinforcement learning. PFRL currently has reproducibility scripts for 11 key deep reinforcement learning algorithms based on original research papers.

As you've seen in this book, PyTorch is a highly customizable framework. This characteristic sometimes results in the need to write the same boilerplate code often for common tasks. To help developers write code faster and eliminate the need for boilerplate code, several PyTorch projects provide high-level programming APIs or compatibility with other high-level frameworks like scikit-learn.

Table 8-4 provides a list of the Ecosystem projects that support *high-level programming*.

Table 8-4. High-level programming projects

Project	Description
fastai	Library that simplifies training using modern practices (*https://pytorch.tips/fastai*)
PyTorch Lightning	Customizable Keras-like ML library that eliminates boilerplate code (*https://pytorch.tips/lightning*)
Ignite	Library for writing compact, full-featured training loops (*https://pytorch.tips/ignite*)
Catalyst	Framework for compact reinforcement learning pipelines (*https://pytorch.tips/catalyst*)
skorch	Provides PyTorch compatibility with scikit-learn (*https://pytorch.tips/skorch*)
Hydra	Framework for configuring complex applications (*https://pytorch.tips/hydra*)

Project	Description
higher	Facilitates the implementation of complex meta-learning algorithms (*https://pytorch.tips/higher*)
Poutyne	Keras-like framework for boilerplate code (*https://pytorch.tips/poutyne*)

Fastai is a research and learning framework built on PyTorch. It has comprehensive documentation and has provided a high-level API for PyTorch since the library's early days. You can get up to speed with the framework quickly by consultng its documentation and free online courses (*https://pytorch.tips/fastai*) or reading the book *Deep Learning for Coders with fastai and PyTorch* (*https://pytorch.tips/fastai-book*) by Jeremy Howard and Sylvain Gugger (O'Reilly).

PyTorch Lightning has also become one a very popular high-level programming API for PyTorch. It provides all the necessary boilerplate code for training, validation, and test loops while allowing you to easily add customizations for your methods.

Ignite and Catalyst are also popular high-level frameworks, while skorch and Poutyne provide scikit-learn and Keras-like interfaces, respectively. Hydra and higher are used to simplify the configuration of complex applications.

In addition to high-level frameworks, there are packages in the Ecosystem that support hardware acceleration and optimized inference.

Table 8-5 provides a list of ecosystem projects that support *inference acceleration* applications.

Table 8-5. Inference projects

Project	Description
Glow	ML compiler for hardware acceleration (*https://pytorch.tips/glow*)
Hummingbird	Compiles trained models for faster inference (*https://pytorch.tips/hummingbird*)

Glow is a machine learning compiler and execution engine for hardware accelerators, and it can be used as a backend for high-level deep learning frameworks. The compiler allows state-of-the-art optimizations and code generation of neural network graphs. Hummingbird is an open source project developed by Microsoft. It is a library for compiling trained, traditional ML models into tensor computations and seamlessly leverages PyTorch to accelerate traditional ML models.

In addition to accelerating inference, the PyTorch Ecosystem also contains projects to accelerate training and optimize models using distributed training.

Table 8-6 provides a list of ecosystem projects that support *distributed training and model optimization*.

Table 8-6. Distributed training and model optimization projects

Project	Description
Ray	Fast, simple framework for building and running distributed applications (*https://pytorch.tips/ray*)
Horovod	Distributed deep learning training framework for TensorFlow, Keras, PyTorch, and Apache MXNet (*https://pytorch.tips/horovod*)
DeepSpeed	Optimization library (*https://pytorch.tips/deepspeed*)
Optuna	Automated hyperparameter search and optimization (*https://pytorch.tips/optuna*)
Polyaxon	Platform for building, training, and monitoring large-scale deep learning applications (*https://pytorch.tips/polyaxon*)
Determined	Platform that trains models using shared GPUs and collaboration (*https://pytorch.tips/determined*)
Allegro Trains	Library that contains a deep learning experiment manager, versioning, and machine learning ops (*https://pytorch.tips/allegro*)

Ray is a Python API for building distributed applications and is packaged with other libraries for accelerating machine learning workloads. We used one of these packages, Ray Tune, in

Chapter 6 to tune hyperparameters on a distributed system. Ray is a very powerful package that can also support scalable reinforcement learning, distributed training, and scalable serving. Horovod is another distributed framework. It is focused on distributed training and can be used with Ray.

DeepSpeed, Optuna, and Allegro Trains also support hyperparameter tuning and model optimization. Polyaxon can be used to train and monitor models at scale, and Determined focuses on sharing GPUs for accelerated training.

With the growth in PyTorch's popularity, there have been quite a few specialized packages developed to support niche domains and specific tools. Many of these tools aim to improve models or the preprocessing of data.

Table 8-7 provides a list of the Ecosystem projects that support *modeling and data processing*.

Table 8-7. Modeling and data processing projects

Project	Description
TensorBoard	TensorBoard's data and model visualization tool is integrated into PyTorch (*https://pytorch.tips/pytorch-tensorboard*)
PyTorch Geometric	Geometric deep learning extension library for PyTorch (*https://pytorch.tips/geometric*)
Pyro	Flexible and extensible deep probabilistic modeling (*https://pytorch.tips/pyro*)
Deep Graph Library (DGL)	Library for implementation of graph neural networks (*https://pytorch.tips/dgl*)
MMF	Facebook's modular framework for multi-model deep learning (vision and language) (*https://pytorch.tips/mmf*)
GPyTorch	Library for creating scalable Gaussian process models (*https://pytorch.tips/gpytorch*)
BoTorch	Library for Bayesian optimization (*https://pytorch.tips/botorch*)
Torch Points 3D	Framework for unstructured 3D spatial data (*https://pytorch.tips/torchpoints3d*)

Project	Description
TensorLy	High level API for tensor methods and deep tensorized neural networks (*https://pytorch.tips/tensorly*) (*https://pytorch.tips/advertorch*)
BaaL	Implements active learning from Bayesian theory (*https://pytorch.tips/baal*)
PennyLane	Library for quantum ML (*https://pytorch.tips/pennylane*)

TensorBoard is a very popular visualization tool developed for TensorFlow that can be used for PyTorch as well. We'll cover this tool and its PyTorch API later in this chapter.

PyTorch Geometric, Pyro, GPyTorch, BoTorch, and BaaL all support different types of modeling, such as geometric, probabilistic, Gaussian modeling, and Bayesian optimization.

Facebook's MMF is a feature-rich package for multi-modal modeling, and Torch Points 3D can be used to model generic 3D spatial data.

PyTorch's maturity and stability as a tool shows in the advent of packages used to support security and privacy. Security and privacy concerns are becoming more important as regulations require systems to be compliant in these domains.

Table 8-8 provides a list of ecosystem projects that support *security and privacy*.

Table 8-8. Security and privacy projects

Project	Description
AdverTorch	Modules for adversarial examples and defending against attacks
PySyft	Library for model encryption and privacy (*https://pytorch.tips/pysyft*)
Opacus	Library for training models with differential privacy (*https://pytorch.tips/opacus*)
CrypTen	Framework for privacy preserving ML (*https://pytorch.tips/crypten*)

PySyft, Opacus, and CrypTen are PyTorch packages that support security and privacy. They add features to protect and encrypt models and the data used to create them.

Often deep learning seems like a black box, where developers have no idea why models make the decisions they make. Today, however, this lack of transparency is no longer acceptable: there is a growing awareness that companies and their executives must be held accountable for the fairness and operations of their algorithms. Model interpretability is important for researchers, developers, and company executives to understand why models produce their results.

Table 8-9 shows the ecosystem project that support *model interpretability*.

Table 8-9. Model interpretability projects

Project	Description
Captum	Library for model interpretability (*https://pytorch.tips/captum*)
Visual attribution	PyTorch implementation of recent visual attribution methods for model interpretability (*https://pytorch.tips/visual-attribution*)

Currently, Captum is the premier PyTorch project that supports model interpretability. The Visual attribution package is useful for interpreting computer vision models and identifying image saliency. As the field expands, more projects are sure to enter this space.

As you can see, the PyTorch Ecosystem includes a broad range of open source projects that can assist you in many different ways. Perhaps you are working on a project that could benefit other researchers. If you'd like to make your project a part of the official PyTorch Ecosystem, visit the PyTorch Ecosystem application page (*https://pytorch.tips/join-ecosystem*).

When considering applications, the PyTorch team looks for projects that meet the following requirements:

- Your project uses PyTorch to improve the user experience, add new capabilities, or speed up training/inference.

- Your project is stable, well maintained, and includes adequate infrastructure, documentation, and technical support.

The Ecosystem is constantly growing. To access the latest list of projects, visit the PyTorch Ecosystem website. (*https://pytorch.tips/ecosystem*) To update us on new projects for the book, please email the author at *jpapa@joepapa.ai*.

Next, we will go a little deeper into some of the PyTorch project's supporting tools and libraries. We obviously can't cover all of the available libraries and tools in this book, but in the following sections we'll explore a few of the most popular and useful ones to give you a deeper understanding of their APIs and usage.

Torchvision for Image and Video

We've used Torchvision through this book, and it is one of the most powerful and useful PyTorch libraries for computer vision research. Technically, the Torchvision package is part of the PyTorch project. It consists of a selection of popular datasets, model architectures, and common image transformations.

Datasets and I/O

Torchvision provides a large assortment of datasets. They are included in the `torchvision.datasets` library and can be accessed by creating a dataset object, as shown in the following code:

```
import torchvision

train_data = torchvision.datasets.CIFAR10(
        root=".",
        train=True,
        transform=None,
        download=True)
```

You simply call the constructor function and pass in the appropriate options. This code creates a dataset object from the CIFAR-10 dataset using the training data with no transforms. It look for the dataset files in the current directory, and if they don't exist, it will download them.

Table 8-10 provides a comprehensive list of datasets available from Torchvision.

Table 8-10. Torchvision datasets

Dataset	Description
CelebA	Large-scale face attributes dataset with more than 200,000 celebrity images, each with 40 attribute annotations.
CIFAR-10	CIFAR-10 dataset consisting of 60,000 32×32 color images in 10 classes, split into 50,000 training and 10,000 test images. The CIFAR-100 dataset, which has 100 classes, is also available.
Cityscapes	Large-scale dataset containing video sequences recorded in street scenes from 50 different cities, with annotations.
COCO	Large-scale object detection, segmentation, and captioning dataset.
DatasetFolder	Used to create any dataset from files in a folder structure.
EMNIST	An extension of MNIST to handwritten letter.
FakeData	A fake dataset that returns randomly generated images as PIL images.
Fashion-MNIST	Dataset of Zalando's clothing images matching the MNIST format (60,000 training examples, 10,000 test examples, 28×28 grayscale images, 10 classes).
Flickr	Flickr 8,000-image dataset.
HMDB51	Large human motion database of video sequences.
ImageFolder	Used to create an image dataset from files in a folder structure.
ImageNet	Image classification dataset with 14,197,122 images and 21,841 word phrases.

Dataset	Description
Kinetics-400	Large-scale action recognition video dataset with 650,000 10-second video clips that cover up to 700 human action classes such as playing instruments, shaking hands, and hugging.
KMNIST	Kuzushiji-MNIST, a drop-in replacement for the MNIST dataset (70,000 28 × 28 grayscale images) where one character represents each of the 10 rows of Hiragana.
LSUN	One million labeled images for each of 10 scene categories and 20 object categories.
MNIST	Handwritten, single-digit numbers as 28 × 28 grayscale images with 60,000 training and 10,000 test samples.
Omniglot	Human-generated dataset of 1,623 different handwritten characters from 50 different alphabets.
PhotoTour	Photo tourism dataset consisting of 1,024 × 1,024 bitmap images, each containing a 16 × 16 array of image patches.
Places365	Dataset of 10 million images comprising 400+ unique scene categories with 5,000 to 30,000 training images per class.
QMNIST	Facebook's project to generate an MNIST dataset from the original data found in the NIST Special Database 19.
SBD	Semantic boundaries dataset that contains annotations from 11,355 images for semantic segmentation.
SBU	Stony Brook University (SBU) captioned photo dataset containing over 1 million captioned images.
STL10	CIFAR-10-like dataset used for unsupervised learning. 10 classes of 96 × 96 color images with 5,000 training, 8,000 test, and 100,000 unlabeled images.
SVHN	Street view house numbers dataset, similar to MNIST but with 10× more data in natural scene color images.
UCF101	Action recognition dataset with 13,320 videos from 101 action categories.
USPS	Dataset of 16 × 16 handwritten text images with 10 classes, 7,291 training and 2,007 test images.

Dataset	Description
VOC	PASCAL visual object classes image datasets for object class recognition. The 2012 version has 20 classes, 11,530 training/validation images with 27,450 region of interest (ROI) annotated objects and 6,929 segmentations.

More datasets are being added to Torchvision all the time. For an up-to-date list, visit the Torchvision documentation (*https://pytorch.tips/torchvision-datasets*).

Models

Torchvision also provides an extensive list of models, containing both the module architectures and pretrained weights if available. The model object is easily created by calling the corresponding constructor function, as shown here:

```
import torchvision

model = torchvision.models.vgg16(pretrained=False)
```

This code creates a VGG16 model with random weights since the pretrained weights are not used. You can instantiate many different computer vision models by using a similar constructor and setting the appropriate parameters. Torchvision provides pretrained models using the PyTorch `torch.utils.model_zoo`. These can be constructed by passing `pretrained=True`.

Table 8-11 provides a comprehensive list of models included in Torchvision, by category. These models are well known in the research community, and the table includes references to the research papers associated with each model.

Table 8-11. Torchvision models

Model	Paper
Classification	
AlexNet	"One Weird Trick for Parallelizing Convolutional Neural Networks," by Alex Krizhevsky

Model	Paper
VGG	"Very Deep Convolutional Networks for Large-Scale Image Recognition," by Karen Simonyan and Andrew Zisserman
ResNet	"Deep Residual Learning for Image Recognition," by Kaiming He et al.
SqueezeNet	"SqueezeNet: AlexNet-Level Accuracy with 50x Fewer Parameters and <0.5MB Model Size," by Forrest N. Iandola et al.
DenseNet	"Densely Connected Convolutional Networks," by Gao Huang et al.
Inception v3	"Rethinking the Inception Architecture for Computer Vision," by Christian Szegedy et al.
GoogLeNet	"Going Deeper with Convolutions," by Christian Szegedy et al.
ShuffleNet v2	"ShuffleNet V2: Practical Guidelines for Efficient CNN Architecture Design," by Ningning Ma et al.
MobileNet v2	"MobileNetV2: Inverted Residuals and Linear Bottlenecks," by Mark Sandler et al.
ResNeXt	"Aggregated Residual Transformations for Deep Neural Networks," by Saining Xie et al.
Wide ResNet	"Wide Residual Networks," by Sergey Zagoruyko and Nikos Komodakis
MNASNet	"MnasNet: Platform-Aware Neural Architecture Search for Mobile," by Mingxing Tan et al.
Semantic segmentation	
FCN ResNet50	"Fully Convolutional Networks for Semantic Segmentation," by Jonathan Long et al.
FCN ResNet101	See above

Model	Paper
DeepLabV3 ResNet50	"Rethinking Atrous Convolution for Semantic Image Segmentation," by Liang-Chieh Chen et al.
DeepLabV3 ResNet101	See above
Object detection	
Faster R-CNN ResNet-50	"FPNFaster R-CNN: Towards Real-Time Object Detection with Region Proposal Networks," by Shaoqing Ren et al.
Mask R-CNN ResNet-50 FPN	"Mask R-CNN," by Kaiming He et al.
Video classification	
ResNet 3D 18	"A Closer Look at Spatiotemporal Convolutions for Action Recognition," by Du Tran et al.
ResNet MC 18	See above
ResNet (2+1)D	See above

New computer vision models are also being added to Torchvision all the time. For an up-to-date list, visit the Torchvision documentation (*https://pytorch.tips/torchvision-models*).

Transforms, Operations, and Utilities

Torchvision also provides a comprehensive collection of transforms, operations, and utilities to assist in image preprocessing and data preparation. A common approach to applying transforms is to form a composition of transforms and pass this transforms object into the dataset constructor function, as shown in the following code:

```
from torchvision import transforms, datasets

train_transforms = transforms.Compose([
                    transforms.ToTensor(),
                    transforms.Normalize(
                    (0.4914, 0.4822, 0.4465),
                    (0.2023, 0.1994, 0.2010)),
                    ])
train_data = datasets.CIFAR10(
```

```
                    root=".",
                    train=True,
                    transform=train_transforms)
```

Here, we create a composite transform that converts the data to a tensor using ToTensor() then normalizes the image data using predetermined means and standard deviations for each channel. Setting the transform parameter to this train_transforms object configures the dataset to apply the sequence of transforms when data is accessed.

Table 8-12 provides a complete list of available transforms from torchvision.transforms. Transforms that appear in *italics* in this and Table 8-13 are currently not supported by TorchScript.

Table 8-12. Torchvision transforms

Transform	Description
Operational transforms	
Compose()	Creates a transform based on a sequence of other transforms
CenterCrop(size)	Crops an image in the center with the given size
ColorJitter(brightness=0, contrast=0, saturation=0, hue=0)	Randomly changes the brightness, contrast, saturation, and hue of an image
FiveCrop(size)	Crops an image into four corners and the center crop
Grayscale(num_output_channels=1)	Converts a color image to grayscale
Pad(*padding*, fill=0, padding_mode=constant)	Pads the edges of an image with the given value
RandomAffine(*degrees*, translate=None, scale=None, shear=None, resample=0, fill color=0)	Randomly applies an affine transformation

Transform	Description
`RandomApply(transforms, p=0.5)`	Randomly applies a list of transforms with a given probability
`RandomCrop(size, padding=None, pad_if_needed=False, fill=0, padding_mode=constant)`	Crops an image at a random location
`RandomGrayscale(p=0.1)`	Randomly converts an image to grayscale with a given probability
`RandomHorizontalFlip(p=0.5)`	Randomly flips an image horizontally with a given probability
`RandomPerspective(distortion_scale=0.5, p=0.5, interpolation=2, fill=0)`	Applies a random perspective transformation
`RandomResizedCrop(size, scale=(0.08, 1.0), ratio=(0.75, 1.3333333333333333), interpolation=2)`	Resizes an image with a random size and aspect ratio
`RandomRotation(degrees, resample=False, expand=False, center=None, fill=None)`	Rotates an image randomly
`RandomVerticalFlip(p=0.5)`	Randomly flips an image vertically with a given probability
`Resize(size, interpolation=2)`	Resizes an image to a random size
`TenCrop(size, vertical_flip=False)`	Crops an image into four corners and the center crop and additionally provides a flipped version of each

Transform	Description
GaussianBlur(kernel_size, sigma=(0.1, 2.0))	Applies a Gaussian blur with a random kernel
Conversion transforms	
ToPILImage(mode=None)	Converts a tensor or numpy.ndarray to a PIL image
ToTensor()	Converts a PIL image or ndarray to a tensor
Generic transforms	
Lambda(lambda)	Applies a user-defined lambda as a transform

Most of the transforms can operate on images in tensor or PIL format with a [..., C, H, W] shape, where ... means an arbitrary number of leading dimensions. However, some transforms only operate on PIL images or tensor image data.

The transforms listed in Table 8-13 operate only on PIL images. These transforms are currently not supported by TorchScript.

Table 8-13. Torchvision PIL-only transforms

Transform	Description
RandomChoice(transforms)	Applies a single transform picked randomly from a list
RandomOrder(transforms)	Applies a sequence of transforms in random order

The transforms listed in Table 8-14 operate only on tensor images.

Table 8-14. Torchvision tensor-only transforms

Transform	Description
`LinearTransformation(` `transformation_matrix,` `mean_vector)`	Applies a linear transformation to a tensor image based on a square transformation matrix and a `mean_vector` computed offline.
`Normalize(mean, std,` `inplace=False)`	Normalizes a tensor image with a given mean and standard deviation.
`RandomErasing(p=0.5,` `scale=(0.02, 0.33),` `ratio=(0.3, 3.3), value=0,` `inplace=False)`	Randomly chooses a rectangle region and erases its pixels.
`ConvertImageDtype(dtype:` `torch.dtype)`	Converts a tensor image to a new data type and automatically scales its values to match the type

---

NOTE

Use `torch.nn.Sequential()` instead of `torchvision.` `transforms.Compose()` when scripting transforms for C++ usage. The following code shows an example:

```
>>> transforms = torch.nn.Sequential(
        transforms.CenterCrop(10),
        transforms.Normalize(
            (0.485, 0.456, 0.406), (0.229, 0.224,
            0.225)),
        )

>>> scripted_transforms = torch.jit.script(transforms)
```

Many of the transforms listed in the previous tables contain a random number generator for specifying the parameter. For example, `RandomResizedCrop()` crops an image to a random size and aspect ratio.

Torchvision also provides functional transforms as part of the torchvision.transforms.functional package. You can use these transforms to perform transformations with a specific set of parameters that you choose. For example, you could call torchvision.transforms.functional.adjust_brightness() to adjust the brightness of one on more images.

Table 8-15 provides a list of the supported functional transforms.

Table 8-15. Torchvision functional transforms

Functional transforms and utilities

```
adjust_brightness(img: torch.Tensor,
brightness_factor: float)
```

```
adjust_contrast(img: torch.Tensor,
contrast_factor: float)
```

```
adjust_gamma(img: torch.Tensor, gamma: float,
gain: float = 1)
```

```
adjust_hue(img: torch.Tensor, hue_factor: float) →
torch.Tensor
```

```
adjust_saturation(img: torch.Tensor,
saturation_factor: float)
```

```
affine(img: torch.Tensor, angle: float,
translate: List[int], scale: float, shear: List[float],
resample: int = 0, fillcolor: Optional[int] = None)
```

```
center_crop(img: torch.Tensor, output_size: List[int])
```

```
convert_image_dtype(image: torch.Tensor,
dtype: torch.dtype = torch.float32)
```

```
crop(img: torch.Tensor, top: int, left: int,
height: int, width: int)
```

```
erase(img: torch.Tensor, i: int, j: int, h: int,
w: int, v: torch.Tensor, inplace: bool = False)
```

```
five_crop(img: torch.Tensor, size: List[int])
```

```
gaussian_blur(img: torch.Tensor, kernel_size:
List[int], sigma: Optional[List[float]] = None)

hflip(img: torch.Tensor)

normalize(tensor: torch.Tensor, mean: List[float],
std: List[float], inplace: bool = False)

pad(img: torch.Tensor, padding: List[int],
fill: int = 0, padding_mode: str = constant)

perspective(img: torch.Tensor, startpoints:
List[List[int]], endpoints: List[List[int]],
interpolation: int = 2, fill: Optional[int] = None)

pil_to_tensor(pic)

resize(img: torch.Tensor, size: List[int],
interpolation: int = 2)

resized_crop(img: torch.Tensor, top: int, left: int,
height: int, width: int, size: List[int],
interpolation: int = 2)

rgb_to_grayscale(img: torch.Tensor,
num_output_channels: int = 1)

rotate(img: torch.Tensor, angle: float,
resample: int = 0, expand: bool = False,
center: Optional[List[int]] = None,
fill: Optional[int] = None)

ten_crop(img: torch.Tensor, size: List[int],
vertical_flip: bool = False)

to_grayscale(img, num_output_channels=1)

to_pil_image(pic, mode=None)

to_tensor(pic)

vflip(img: torch.Tensor)
```

```
utils.save_image(tensor: Union[torch.Tensor,
List[torch.Tensor]], fp: Union[str, pathlib.Path,
BinaryIO], nrow: int = 8, padding: int = 2, normalize:
bool = False, range: Optional[Tuple[int, int]] =
None, scale_each: bool = False, pad_value: int = 0,
format: Optional[str] = None)

utils.make_grid(tensor: Union[torch.Tensor,
List[torch.Tensor]], nrow: int = 8, padding: int = 2,
normalize: bool = False, range: Optional[Tuple[int,
int]] = None, scale_each: bool = False,
pad_value: int = 0)
```

As you can see in the table above, Torchvision provides a robust set of functional operations that you can use to process your image data. Each one has its own set of parameters for robust control.

In addition, Torchvision provides functions to facilitate I/O and operations. Table 8-16 provides a list of some of these functions.

Table 8-16. Torchvision functions for I/O and operations

Function

Video

```
io.read_video(filename: str, start_pts: int = 0,
end_pts: Optional[float] = None, pts_unit: str = pts)

io.read_video_timestamps9filename: str, pts_unit: str
= pts)

io.write_video9filename: str, video_array:
torch.Tensor, _fps: float, video_codec: str = libx264,
options: Optional[Dict[str, Any]] = None)
```

Fine-grained video

```
io.VideoReader(path, stream=video)
```

Function

Image

```
io.decode_image(input: torch.Tensor)

io.encode_jpeg(input: torch.Tensor, quality: int = 75)

io.read_image(path: str)

io.write_jpeg(input: torch.Tensor, filename: str,
quality: int = 75)

io.encode_png(input: torch.Tensor, compression_level:
int = 6)

io.write_png(input: torch.Tensor, filename: str,
compression_level: int = 6)
```

The preceding functions are provided so that you can quickly read and write video and image files in multiple formats. They allow you to speed up your image and video processing without the need to write these functions from scratch.

As you can see, Torchvision is a feature-rich, well-supported, and mature PyTorch package. This section provided a quick reference to the Torchvision API. In the next section, we'll explore another popular PyTorch package for NLP and text applications called Torchtext.

Torchtext for NLP

The Torchtext package consists of a collection of data-processing utilities and popular datasets for NLP. The Torchtext API is slightly different from the Torchvision API, but the overall approach is the same.

Create a Dataset Object

First you create a dataset and describe a preprocessing pipeline, as we did with Torchvision transforms. Torchtext provides a set of well-known datasets out of the box. For example, we can load the IMDb dataset as shown in the following code:

```
from torchtext.datasets import IMDB

train_iter, test_iter = \
  IMDB(split=('train', 'test'))

next(train_iter)
# out:
# ('neg',
# 'I rented I AM CURIOUS-YELLOW ...)
```

We automatically create an iterator and can access the data
using next().

WARNING

Torchtext significantly changed its API in PyTorch 1.8. If
the code in this section returns errors, you may need to
upgrade your version of PyTorch.

Preprocess Data

Torchtext also provides features to preprocess text and create
data pipelines. Preprocessing tasks may include defining tokenizers, vocabularies, and numerical embeddings.

In the new Torchtext API, you can access different tokenizers
using the data.get_tokenizer() function, as shown in the following code:

```
from torchtext.data.utils \
  import get_tokenizer

tokenizer = get_tokenizer('basic_english')
```

Creating vocabularies in the new API is also flexible. You can
build a vocabulary directly with the Vocab class, as shown in the
following code:

```
from collections import Counter
from torchtext.vocab import Vocab

train_iter = IMDB(split='train')
counter = Counter()
```

```
for (label, line) in train_iter:
    counter.update(tokenizer(line))
vocab = Vocab(counter,
              min_freq=10,
              specials=('<unk>',
                        '<BOS>',
                        '<EOS>',
                        '<PAD>'))
```

As you can see, we can set the `min_freq` to specify the cutoff frequency in the vocabulary. We can also assign tokens to special symbols like `<BOS>` and `<EOS>`, as shown in the constructor of the `Vocab` class.

Another useful feature is to define transforms for text and labels, as shown in the following code:

```
text_transform = lambda x: [vocab['<BOS>']] \
  + [vocab[token] \
    for token in tokenizer(x)] + [vocab['<EOS>']]

label_transform = lambda x: 1 \
  if x == 'pos' else 0

print(text_transform("programming is awesome"))
# out: [1, 8320, 12, 1156, 2]
```

We pass in a text string to our transforms, and we use the vocabulary and tokenizer to preprocess the data.

Create a Dataloader for Batching

Now that we have loaded and preprocessed our data, the last step is to create a dataloader to sample and batch data from the dataset. We can create a dataloader with the following code:

```
from torch.utils.data import DataLoader

train_iter = IMDB(split='train')
train_dataloader = DataLoader(
    list(train_iter),
    batch_size=8,
    shuffle=True)

# for text, label in train_dataloader
```

You may notice that this code is similar to the code with which we created a dataloader in Torchvision. Instead of passing in the dataset object, we pass the `train_iter` cast as a `list()`. The `DataLoader()` constructor also accepts `batch_sampler` and `col late_fcn` parameters (not shown in the preceding code; see the documentation (*https://pytorch.tips/data*)) so you can customize how the dataset is sampled and collated. After you create the dataloader, use it to train your model, as shown in the preceding code comments.

Torchtext has many useful features. Let's explore what's available from the API.

Data (torchtext.data)

The `torchtext.data` API provides functions for creating text-based dataset objects in PyTorch. Table 8-17 lists the available functions in `torchtext.data`.

Table 8-17. Torchtext data

Function	Description
torchtext.data.utils	
get_tokenizer(*tokenizer, language=en*)	Generates a tokenizer function for a string sentence
ngrams_iterator(*token_ list, ngrams*)	Returns an iterator that yields the given tokens and their ngrams
torchtext.data.functional	
generate_sp_model(*filename, vocab_size=20000, model_type=unigram, model_prefix=m_user*)	Trains a SentencePiece tokenizer
load_sp_model(*spm*)	Loads a SentencePiece model from a file

Function	Description
`sentencepiece_numericalizer(sp_model)`	Creates a generator that takes in a text sentence and outputs the corresponding identifiers based on a `SentencePiece` model
`sentencepiece_tokenizer(sp_model)`	Creates a generator that takes in a text sentence and outputs the corresponding tokens based on a `SentencePiece` model
`custom_replace(replace_pattern)`	Acts as a transform to convert text strings
`simple_space_split(iterator)`	Acts as a transform to split text strings by spaces
`numericalize_tokens_from_iterator(vocab, iterator, removed_tokens=None)`	Yields a list of identifiers from a token iterator with a vocab
`torchtext.data.metrics`	
`bleu_score(candidate_corpus, references_corpus, max_n=4, weights=[0.25, 0.25, 0.25, 0.25])`	Computes the BLEU score between a candidate translation corpus and a reference translation corpus

As you can see, the `torchtext.data` submodule supports functions for creating dataset objects based on fields aas well as for loading, preprocessing, and iterating through batches. Next let's see what NLP datasets are available from the Torchtext library.

Datasets (torchtext.datasets)

Torchtext supports loading datasets from popular papers and research. You can find datasets for language modeling, sentiment analysis, text classification, question classification, entailment, machine translation, sequence tagging, question answering, and unsupervised learning.

Table 8-18 provides a comprehensive list of the datasets included in Torchtext.

Table 8-18. Torchtext datasets

Function	Description
Text classification	
TextClassificationDataset(*vocab, data, labels*)	Generic text-classification dataset
IMDB(*root=.data, split=(train, test)*)	Binary sentiment analysis dataset consisting of 50,000 reviews labeled as positive or negative from IMDb
AG_NEWS(*root=.data, split=(train, test)*)	Dataset of news articles labeled with four topics
SogouNews(*root=.data, split=(train, test)*)	Dataset of news articles labeled with five topics
DBpedia(*root=.data, split=(train, test)*)	Dataset of news articles labeled with 14 categories
YelpReviewPolarity(*root=.data, split=(train, test)*)	Dataset of 500,000 Yelp reviews with binary classification
YelpReviewFull(*root=.data, split=(train, test)*)	Dataset of 500,000 Yelp reviews with fine-grained (five-class) classification
YahooAnswers(*root=.data, split=(train, test)*)	Dataset of Yahoo answers labeled in 10 different categories
AmazonReviewPolarity(*root=.data, split=(train, test)*)	Dataset of Amazon reviews with binary classification

Function	Description
`AmazonReviewFull(`*root=.data,* *split=(train, test)*`)`	Dataset of Amazon reviews with fine-grained (five-class) classification

Language modeling

Function	Description
`LanguageModelingDataset(`*path,* *text_field, newline_eos=True,* *encoding=utf-8, **kwargs*`)`	General language modeling dataset class
`WikiText2(`*root=.data,* *split=(train, valid, test)*`)`	WikiText long-term dependency language modeling dataset, a collection of over 100 million tokens extracted from the set of verified "Good" and "Featured" articles on Wikipedia
`WikiText103(`*root=.data,* *split=(train, valid, test)*`)`	Larger WikiText dataset
`PennTreebank(`*root=.data,* *split=(train, valid, test)*`)`	A relatively small dataset originally created for part of speech (POS) tagging

Machine translation

Function	Description
`TranslationDataset(`*path, exts,* *fields, **kwargs*`)`	Generic translation dataset class
`IWSLT2016(`*root=.data,* *split=(train, valid, test),* *language_pair=(de, en),* *valid_set=tst2013,* *test_set=tst2014*`)`	International Conference on Spoken Language Translation (IWSLT) 2016 TED talk translation task
`IWSLT2017(`*root=.data,* *split=(train, valid, test),* *language_pair=(de, en)*`)`	International Conference on Spoken Language Translation (IWSLT) 2017 TED talk translation task

Function	Description
Sequence tagging	
`SequenceTaggingDataset(path, fields, encoding=utf-8, separator=t, **kwargs)`	Generic sequence-tagging dataset class
`UDPOS(root=.data, split=(train, valid, test))`	Universal dependencies version 2 POS-tagged data
`CoNLL2000Chunking(root=.data, split=(train, test))`	Command that downloads and loads the Conference on Computational Natural Language Learning (CoNLL) 2000 chunking dataset
Question answering	
`SQuAD1(root=.data, split=(train, dev))`	Creates the Stanford Question Answering Dataset (SQuAD) 1.0 dataset, a reading comprehension dataset consisting of questions posed by crowdworkers on a set of Wikipedia articles
`SQuAD2(root=.data, split=(train, dev))`	Creates the Stanford Question Answering Dataset (SQuAD) 2.0 dataset, a dataset that extends the 1.0 dataset by adding over 50,000 unanswerable questions

Torchtext developers are always adding new datasets. For the most updated list, visit the Torchtext datasets documentation (*https://pytorch.tips/torchtext-datasets*).

Once you load data, whether from existing datasets or ones that you create, you will need to convert the text data to numeric data before training a model and running inference. To do so, we use vocabularies and word embeddings that provide the maps to perform these conversions. Next, we'll examine the Torchtext functions used to support vocabularies.

Vocabularies (torchtext.vocab)

Torchtext provides generic classes and specific classes for popular vocabularies. Table 8-19 provides a list of classes in torch text.vocab to support the creation and use of vocabularies.

Table 8-19. Torchtext vocabularies

Function	Description
Vocabulary classes	
Vocab(counter, max_size=None, min_freq=1, specials=(<unk>, <pad>), vectors=None, unk_init=None, vectors_cache=None, specials_first=True)	Defines a vocabulary object that will be used to numericalize a field
SubwordVocab(counter, max_size=None, specials=<pad>, vectors=None, unk_init=<method zero_of torch._C._TensorBase objects>)	Creates a revtok subword vocabulary from a collections.Counter
Vectors(name, cache=None, url=None, unk_init=None, max_vectors=None)	Generic class for word vector embeddings
Pretrained word embeddings	
GloVe(name=840B, dim=300, **kwargs)	Global vectors (GloVe) model for distributed word representation, developed at Stanford
FastText(language=en, **kwargs)	Pretrained word embeddings for 294 languages, created by Facebook's AI Research lab

Function	Description
CharNGram(**kwargs)	CharNGram embeddings, a simple approach for learning character-based compositional models to embed textual sequences
Miscellaneous	
build_vocab_from_iterator(iterator, num_lines=None)	Builds a vocabulary by cycling through an iterator

As you can see, Torchtext provides a robust set of functionality to support text-based modeling and NLP research. For more information, visit the Torchtext documentation (*https:// pytorch.tips/torchtext*).

Whether you're developing deep learning models for NLP, computer vision, or another field, it's helpful to be able to visualize models, data, and performance metrics as you go. In the next section, we'll explore another powerful package for visualization called TensorBoard.

TensorBoard for Visualization

TensorBoard is a visualization toolkit that's included in PyTorch's major competing deep learning framework, Tensor-Flow. Instead of developing its own visualization toolkit, PyTorch integrates with TensorBoard and leverages its visualization capabilities natively.

With TensorBoard, you can visualize learning curves, scalar data, model architectures, weight distributions, and 3D data embeddings, as well as keep track of hyperparameter experiment results. This section will show you how to use Tensor-Board with PyTorch and provide a reference to the Tensor-Board API.

The TensorBoard application is run on a local or remote server, and the display and user interface run in a browser. We can also run TensorBoard inside Jupyter Notebook or Google Colab.

I'll use Colab in this book to demonstrate the capabilities of TensorBoard, but the process is very similar for running it locally or remotely in the cloud. Colab comes with Tensor-Board preinstalled, and you can run it directly in a cell using magic commands, as shown in the following code:

```
%load_ext tensorboard
%tensorboard --logdir ./runs/
```

First we load the `tensorboard` extension and then we run `tensorboard` and specify the log directory that holds the event files. Event files hold the data from PyTorch that will be displayed in the TensorBoard application.

Since we haven't created any event files yet, you will see an empty display, as shown in Figure 8-1.

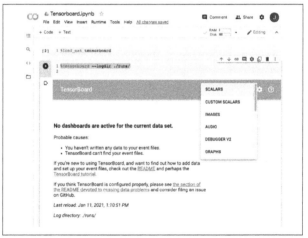

Figure 8-1. TensorBoard application

By clicking on the arrow next to INACTIVE in the upper-right menu, you will see the possible display tabs. One commonly used display tab is the SCALARS tab. This tab can display any scalar value over time. We often use the SCALARS display to view loss and accuracy training curves. Let's see how you can save scalar values for TensorBoard in your PyTorch code.

NOTE

The PyTorch integration with TensorBoard was originally implemented by an open source project called TensorBoardX. Since then, TensorBoard support has been integrated into the PyTorch project as the `torch.utils.tensorboard` package and it's actively maintained by the PyTorch development team.

First let's import PyTorch's TensorBoard interface and set up PyTorch for use with TensorBoard, as shown in the following code:

```
from torch.utils.tensorboard import SummaryWriter

writer = SummaryWriter()  ❶
```

❶ The writer will output to the *./runs/* directory by default.

We simply import the `SummaryWriter` class from the PyTorch `tensorboard` package and instantiate a `SummaryWriter` object. To write data to TensorBoard, all we need to do is call methods from the `SummaryWriter` object. To save our loss values while our model is training, we use the `add_scalar()` method, as shown in the following code:

```
N_EPOCHS = 10
for epoch in range(N_EPOCHS):

    epoch_loss = 0.0
    for inputs, labels in trainloader:
        inputs = inputs.to(device)
        labels = labels.to(device)

        optimizer.zero_grad()

        outputs = model(inputs)
        loss = criterion(outputs, labels)
```

```
        loss.backward()
        optimizer.step()

        epoch_loss += loss.item()
    print("Epoch: {} Loss: {}".format(epoch,
        epoch_loss/len(trainloader)))
    writer.add_scalar('Loss/train',
        epoch_loss/len(trainloader), epoch) ❶
```

❶ Log loss.item() as an event to tensorboard.

This is just an example training loop. You can assume the model has already been defined and the trainloader has been created. Not only does the code print the loss every epoch, but it also logs it to a tensorboard event. We can either refresh the Tensor-Board application in the previous cell or create another cell altogether using the %tensorboard command.

Learning Curves with SCALARS

TensorBoard provides the ability to plot one or more scalar values over time. This is useful in deep learning development to display metrics as your model trains. By viewing metrics like loss or accuracy it's easy to see if your model's training is stable and continues to improve.

Figure 8-2 shows an example display of learning curves using TensorBoard.

You can interact with the display by sliding the smoothing factor, and you can also see the curve at each epoch by mousing over the plots. TensorBoard allows you to apply smoothing to iron out instabilities and show the overall progress.

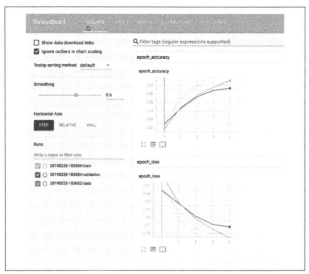

Figure 8-2. TensorBoard learning curves

Model Architectures with GRAPHS

Another useful feature of TensorBoard is visualizing your deep learning model using graphs. To save a graph to the event file, we will use the add_graph() method, as shown in the following code:

```
model = vgg16(preTrained=True)
writer.add_graph(model)
```

In this code we instantiate a VGG16 model and write the model to an event file. We can display the model graph by either refreshing an existing TensorBoard cell or creating a new one. Figure 8-3 shows the graph visualization tool in TensorBoard.

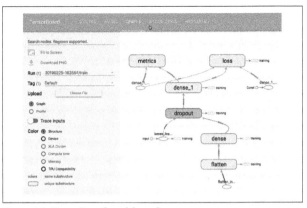

Figure 8-3. TensorBoard model graph

The graph is interactive. You can click on each module and expand it to view the underlying modules. This tool is useful for understanding existing models and verifying that your model graphs match their intended designs.

Data with IMAGES, TEXT, and PROJECTOR

You can also use TensorBoard to view different types of data, such as images, text, and 3D embeddings. In these cases, you would use the add_image(), add_text(), and add_projection() methods, respectively, to write data to the event file.

Figure 8-4 shows a batch of image data from the Fashion-MNIST dataset.

By examining batches of image data, you can verify that the data looks as expected or identify errors in your data or results. TensorBoard also provides the ability to listen to audio data, display text data, and view 3D projections of multidimensional data or data embeddings.

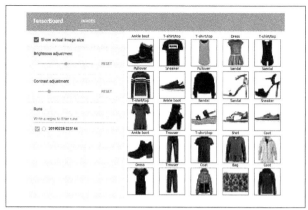

Figure 8-4. TensorBoard image display

Weight Distributions with DISTRIBUTIONS and HISTOGRAMS

Another useful feature of TensorBoard is the ability to display distributions and histograms. This allows you to view large amounts of data to verify expected behavior or identify issues.

One common task in model development is making sure you avoid the *vanishing gradient problem*. Vanishing gradients occur when the model weights become zero or close to zero. When this occurs the neurons essentially die off and can no longer be updated.

If we visualize the distribution of our weights, it's easy to see when a large portion of the weight values have reached zero.

Figure 8-5 shows the DISTRIBUTIONS tab in TensorBoard. Here we can examine the distributions of our weight values.

As you see in Figure 8-5, TensorBoard can display distributions in 3D so it's easy to see how the distributions change over time or over each epoch.

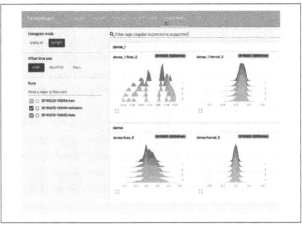

Figure 8-5. TensorBoard weight distributions

Hyperparameters with HPARAMS

When running deep learning experiments, it's easy to lose track of the different hyperparameter sets used to try a hypothesis. TensorBoard provides a way to keep track of the hyperparameter values during each experiment and tabularizes the values and their results.

Figure 8-6 displays an example of how we track experiments and their corresponding hyperparameters and results.

In the HPARAMS tab, you can view the results in table view, parallel coordinates view, or scatter plot matrix view. Each experiment is identified by its session group name, hyperparameters such as dropout percentage and optimizer algorithm, and the resulting metric, such as accuracy. The HPARAMS tables help you keep track of your experiments and results.

When you're finished writing data to TensorBoard event files, you should use the `close()` method, as shown here:

```
writer.close()
```

This will call the destructor function and release any memory that was used for the summary writer.

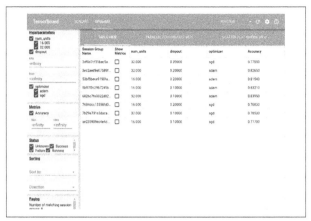

Figure 8-6. TensorBoard hyperparameter tracking

The TensorBoard API

The PyTorch TensorBoard API is pretty simple. It's included as part of the `torch.utils` package as `torch.utils.tensorboard`. Table 8-20 shows a comprehensive list of functions used to interface PyTorch to TensorBoard.

Table 8-20. PyTorch TensorBoard API

Method	Description
`SummaryWriter(log_dir=None, comment='', purge_step=None, max_queue=10, flush_secs=120, filename_suffix='')`	Creates a Summary Writer object
`flush()`	Flushes the event file to disk; makes sure that all pending events have been written to disk

Method	Description
`close()`	Frees the `Summary Writer` object and closes event files
`add_scalar(tag, scalar_value, global_step=None, walltime=None)`	Writes a scalar to the event file
`add_scalars(main_tag, tag_scalar_dict, global_step=None, walltime=None)`	Writes multiple scalars to the event file to display multiple scalars on the same plot
`add_custom_scalars(layout)`	Creates a special chart by collecting chart tags in scalars
`add_histogram(tag, values, global_step=None, bins=tensorflow, walltime=None, max_bins=None)`	Writes data for a histogram display
`add_image(tag, img_tensor, global_step=None, walltime=None, dataformats=CHW)`	Writes image data
`add_images(tag, img_tensor, global_step=None, walltime=None, dataformats=NCHW)`	Writes multiple images to the same display
`add_figure(tag, figure, global_step=None, close=True, walltime=None)`	Writes a `matplotlib`-type plot as an image
`add_video(tag, vid_tensor, global_step=None, fps=4, walltime=None)`	Writes a video
`add_audio(tag, snd_tensor, global_step=None, sample_rate=44100, walltime=None)`	Writes an audio file to the event summary
`add_text(tag, text_string, global_step=None, walltime=None)`	Writes text data to summary

Method	Description
`add_graph(model, input_to_model=None, verbose=False)`	Writes a model graph or computational graph to summary
`add_embedding(mat, metadata=None, label_img=None, global_step=None, tag=default, metadata_header=None)`	Writes embedding projector data tto summary
`add_pr_curve(tag, labels, predictions, global_step=None, num_thresholds=127, weights=None, walltime=None)`	Writes the precision/recall curve under different thresholds
`add_mesh(tag, vertices, colors=None, faces=None, config_dict=None, global_step=None, walltime=None)`	Adds meshes or 3D point clouds to TensorBoard
`add_hparams(hparam_dict, metric_dict, hparam_domain_discrete=None, run_name=None)`	Adds a set of hyperparameters for comparison in TensorBoard

As shown in Table 8-20, the API is simple. You can use the `Sum maryWriter()`, `flush()`, and `close()` methods to manage the writer object and use the other functions to add data to the TensorBoard event file.

For more details on the TensorBoard PyTorch API, visit the TensorBoard API documentation (*https://pytorch.tips/pytorch-tensorboard*). For more details on using the TensorBoard application itself, visit the TensorBoard documentation (*https://pytorch.tips/tensorboard*).

TensorBoard solves one major challenge with developing deep learning models in PyTorch by providing a visualization tool. Another major challenge is keeping up with the latest research and state-of-the art solutions. Researchers often need to reproduce the results and leverage the code for benchmarking their own designs. In the next section we explore Papers with Code, a resource you can use to solve this problem.

Papers with Code

Papers with Code (PwC) is a website that organizes access to machine learning research papers and their corresponding code, which is often written in PyTorch. PwC allows you to easily reproduce experiments and extend current research, and the website allows you to find the best-performing research papers for a given machine learning topic. For example, want to find the best image classification models and their code? Just click on the Image Classification tile and you'll see a summary of the research area as well as benchmarks and links to corresponding papers and code on GitHub. Figure 8-7 shows an example listing for Image Classification.

Figure 8-7. Papers with Code

PwC is not an exclusive PyTorch project; however, most of the code provided on PwC uses PyTorch. It may be able to help you build awareness of the current state-of-the-art research and solve your problems in deep learning and AI. Explore more at the PwC website (*https://pytorch.tips/pwc*).

Additional PyTorch Resources

After reading this book, you should have a good understanding of PyTorch and its features. However, there are always new aspects to explore and practice. In this section, I'll provide a list of additional resources that you can check out to learn more and grow your skills with PyTorch.

Tutorials

The PyTorch website (*https://pytorch.tips/pytorch*) provides an extensive set of documentation and tutorials. If you're looking for more code examples, this resource is a good place to start. Figure 8-8 shows the PyTorch Tutorials website (*https://pytorch.tips/tutorials*), where you can select tags to help you find tutorials that interest you.

Figure 8-8. PyTorch Tutorials

The site includes a 60-min blitz, PyTorch recipes, tutorials, and a PyTorch Cheat Sheet. Most of the code and tutorials are available on GitHub, and can be run in VS Code, Jupyter Notebook, and Colab.

The 60-min Blitz is a good place to start, refresh your skills, or review the basics of PyTorch. PyTorch recipes are bite-sized, actionable examples of how to use specific PyTorch features. PyTorch tutorials are slightly longer than recipes and are composed of multiple steps to achieve or demonstrate an outcome.

Currently, you can find tutorials related to the following topics:

- Audio
- Best Practice
- C++
- CUDA
- Extending PyTorch
- FX
- Frontend APIs
- Getting Started
- Image/Video
- Interpretability
- Memory Format
- Mobile
- Model Optimization
- Parallel and Distributed Training
- Production
- Profiling
- Quantization
- Reinforcement Learning
- TensorBoard
- Text
- TorchScript

The PyTorch team is continually adding new resources and this list is certainly subject to change. For more information and the latest tutorials, visit the PyTorch Tutorials website.

Books

Tutorials are a great for learning, but perhaps you'd prefer to read more about PyTorch and gain different perspectives from multiple authors. Table 8-21 provides a list of other books related to PyTorch.

Table 8-21. PyTorch books

Book	Publisher, year	Summary
Cloud Native Machine Learning by Carl Osipov	Manning, 2021	Learn how to deploy PyTorch models on AWS
Deep Learning for Coders with fastai and PyTorch by Jeremy Howard and Sylvain Gugger	O'Reilly, 2020	Learn how to build AI applications without a PhD
Deep Learning with PyTorch by Eli Stevens et al.	Manning, 2019	Learn how to build, train, and tune NNs using Python tools
Deep Learning with PyTorch by Vishnu Subramanian	Packt, 2018	Learn how to build NN models using PyTorch
Hands-On Generative Adversarial Networks with PyTorch 1.x by John Hany and Greg Walters	Packt, 2019	Learn how to implement next-generation NNs to build powerful GAN models using Python
Hands-On Natural Language Processing with PyTorch 1.x by Thomas Dop	Packt, 2020	Learn how to build smart, AI-driven linguistic applications using deep learning and NLP techniques
Hands-On Neural Networks with PyTorch 1.0 by Vihar Kurama	Packt, 2019	Learn how to implement deep learning architectures in PyTorch
Natural Language Processing with PyTorch by Delip Rao and Brian McMahan	O'Reilly, 2019	Learn how to build intelligent language applications using deep learning

Book	Publisher, year	Summary
Practical Deep Learning with PyTorch by Nihkil Ketkar	Apress, 2020	Learn how to optimize GANs with Python
Programming PyTorch for Deep Learning by Ian Pointer	O'Reilly, 2019	Learn how to create and deploy deep learning applications
PyTorch Artificial Intelligence Fundamentals by Jibin Mathew	Packt, 2020	Learn how to design, build, and deploy your own AI models with PyTorch 1.x
PyTorch Recipes by Pradeepta Mishra	Apress, 2019	Learn how to solve problems in PyTorch

Online Courses and Live Training

If you prefer online video courses and live training workshops, there are options available for you to expand your PyTorch knowledge and skills. You can continue learning from me and other online instructors at PyTorch Academy, Udemy, Coursera, Udacity, Skillshare, DataCamp, Pluralsight, edX, O'Reilly Learning, and LinkedIn Learning. Some courses are free while others require a fee or a subscription.

Table 8-22 lists a selection of online courses on PyTorch available at the time of writing.

Table 8-22. PyTorch courses

Course	Instructor	Platform
Getting Started with PyTorch Development	Joe Papa	PyTorch Academy (*https://pytorch academy.com*)
PyTorch Fundamentals	Joe Papa	PyTorch Academy (*https://pytorch academy.com*)
Advanced PyTorch	Joe Papa	PyTorch Academy (*https://pytorch academy.com*)

Course	Instructor	Platform
Introduction to Deep Learning with PyTorch	Ismail Elezi	DataCamp (*https://www.data camp.com/courses/deep-learning-with-pytorch*)
Foundations of PyTorch	Janani Ravi	Pluralsight (*https://www.plural sight.com/courses/foundations-pytorch*)
Deep Neural Networks with PyTorch	IBM	Coursera (*https://www.cour sera.org/learn/deep-neural-networks-with-pytorch*)
PyTorch Basics for Machine Learning	IBM	edX (*https://www.edx.org/ course/pytorch-basics-for-machine-learning*)
Intro to Deep Learning with PyTorch	Facebook AI	Udacity (*https://www.udac ity.com/course/deep-learning-pytorch—ud188*)
PyTorch: Deep Learning and Artificial Intelligence	Lazy Programmer	Udemy (*https:// www.udemy.com/course/pytorch-deep-learning/*)
PyTorch for Deep Learning and Computer Vision	Rayan Slim et al.	Udemy (*https:// www.udemy.com/course/pytorch-for-deep-learning-and-computer-vision*)
PyTorch for Beginners	Dan We	Skillshare (*https://www.skill share.com/classes/Pytorch-for-beginners-how-machine-learning-with-pytorch-really-works/1042152565*)
PyTorch Essential Training: Deep Learning	Jonathan Fernandes	LinkedIn Learning (*https:// www.linkedin.com/learning/ pytorch-essential-training-deep-learning*)

Course	Instructor	Platform
Introduction to Deep Learning Using PyTorch	Goku Mohandas and Alfredo Canziani	O'Reilly Learning (*https://learn ing.oreilly.com/videos/ introduction-to-deep/ 9781491989944/*)

This chapter has provided resources for expanding your learning, research, and development with PyTorch. You can use this material as a quick reference for the numerous packages within the PyTorch project and the PyTorch Ecosystem. When you are looking to expand your skills and knowledge, you can return to this chapter to get ideas on other training materials available to you.

Congratulations on completing the book! You've come a long way, getting to grips with tensors, understanding the model development process, and exploring reference designs using PyTorch. In addition, you've learned how to customize PyTorch, create your own features, accelerate training, optimize your models, and deploy your NNs to the cloud and edge devices. Finally, we explored the PyTorch Ecosystem, investigated key packages like Torchvision, Torchtext, and TensorBoard, and learned about additional ways to expand your knowledge with tutorials, books, and online courses.

No matter what projects you tackle in the future, I hope you'll be able to return to this book again and again. I also hope you continue to expand your skills and master PyTorch's capabilities to develop innovative new deep learning tools and systems. Don't let your new knowledge and skills dwindle away. Go build something interesting, and make a difference in the world!

Let me know what you create! I hope to see you in one of my courses at PyTorch Academy (*https://pytorchacademy.com*) and feel free to reach out to me via email (*jpapa@joepapa.ai*), Twitter (@JoePapaAI), or LinkedIn (@MrJoePapa).

Index

About the Author

Joe Papa has over 25 years of experience in research and development and is the founder of TeachMe.AI. He holds an MSEE and has led AI research teams with PyTorch at Booz Allen Hamilton and Perspecta Labs. Joe has mentored hundreds of data scientists and has taught more than 6,000 students across the world on Udemy.

Colophon

The animal on the cover of *PyTorch Pocket Reference* is fish in the *Cyclopteridae* family, commonly known as a lumpsucker fish. There are around 30 species in 7 genera known as lumpsuckers. They are found in the cold northern waters of the Arctic, Atlantic, and Pacific Oceans.

The lumpsuckers are named for the adhesive discs behind their pectoral fins. They live near the seabed and use these discs to adhere to rocky substrates, where they feed on invertebrates, crustaceans, and mollusks.

The only species of lumpsucker targeted commercially is *Cyclopterus lumpus*, which has a conservation status of near threatened. Many of the animals on O'Reilly covers are endangered; all of them are important to the world.

The cover illustration is by Karen Montgomery, based on a black and white engraving from *Lydekker's Royal Natural History*. The cover fonts are Gilroy Semibold and Guardian Sans. The text font is Adobe Minion Pro; the heading font is Adobe Myriad Condensed; and the code font is Dalton Maag's Ubuntu Mono.